# SOMEWHERE

×

"Elsewhere: Somewhere"
Various
First Published 2012

Published by Cargo Publishing & McSweeney's
978-1-908885-07-4

Bic Code-FA Modern & Contemporary Fiction
FYB Short Stories

Published in association with the Edinburgh International Book Festival, with the support of Creative Scotland and the Scottish Government's Edinburgh Festivals Expo Fund.

Also available as:
Ebook
Kindle ebook

Printed & bound in China by Shanghai Offset Printing Products Ltd.
Cover illustrations by Jack Teagle
Designed by McSweeney's

www.cargopublishing.com
www.mcsweeneys.net
www.edbookfest.co.uk
www.jackteagle.co.uk

# A FLASH OF BLUE LIGHT

## *by* MICHEL FABER

'I WAS ABDUCTED by aliens,' the woman with the foreign accent told the policeman at the desk.

'Raped?' he suggested hopefully, not because he was a prurient man but because he was keen to offload her onto a female colleague if possible.

'No,' the woman said, narrowing her eyes. 'They didn't have... the equipment.'

Suppressing a yawn, the officer checked the time on his computer screen. It was 3.22. In the morning. There was only one WPC at the station and she was having a kip in the strip search room.

'OK,' he said. 'What's your full name, age, and address, please?'

'My name is Jutta Mollo,' the woman replied calmly. 'I am

thirty-seven. I live at Jahnstrasse 19/A, 3015 Wennigsen 5, near Hanover, Germany.'

The policeman had to get Mrs Mollo to spell out much of this information, since he was Huddersfield-born and his office was in Wombwell, South Yorkshire, where Germans were not abundant.

'What are you doing so far from home?' he enquired.

Ms Mollo ran a dainty – if somewhat grubby – hand through her stylish hairdo. Small fragments of leaf and dandelion fluttered down. 'It's not so far,' she said. 'Compared to last week, when I was a thousand light-years from Earth, I'm very close to Hanover.'

'Still...' said the policeman wearily, waving his hand toward the remaining few hundred miles.

'If you think about it,' the woman persisted, 'the aliens' navigational technology is highly efficient. Out of all the planets in this galaxy, they returned me not just to Earth, but even to Europe.'

'England is not Europe,' said the policeman.

'Yes, we know you don't think so, but, as a matter of fact...'

'Madam,' the policeman sighed. 'What's your problem, *really*?'

A flinty glint appeared in Ms Mollo's blue-grey eyes. 'I was abducted by aliens. Abduction is a crime,' she reminded the officer.

'We've a limited jurisdiction here,' he explained, deadpan. 'We can't go chasing criminals far afield. Sheffield, Leeds, Manchester maybe. Not other solar systems.'

The woman treated his note of flippancy with the severity it deserved.

'My children,' she said, 'are still on the aliens' planet. They returned *me*, but kept them.'

'Now why do you think they did that?'

'They said the children were fresher and more compact. Little Rosi is particularly small.'

The officer examined Mrs Mollo's expression for authenticating signs of emotion. There were none.

'Aside from your say-so,' he said, 'do you have any proof of any of this?'

She sighed. 'I can see I was foolish not to tear off a large hunk of the aliens' spacecraft and conceal it in my underwear. However, this –' (she handed him a slip of paper) '– is the telephone number of my husband in Wennigsen. He will confirm that I disappeared in a flash of blue light at 11.45PM last Wednesday.'

The policeman dialled the number, reasoning that at half past three in the morning it wouldn't cost too much. The phone was picked up instantly at the other end. A strained, breathless male voice said, 'Ja? Mit Dieter Mollo.'

'It's PC Broadbent here, at the constabulary in Wombwell, Yorkshire. It's in connection with your wife and children.'

'I vill pay anysing what you ask,' volunteered Mr Mollo. 'Please do mein femmily no harm.'

Broadbent covered the mouthpiece with his hand and looked over to Mrs Mollo.

'Your husband's English is nowhere near as good as yours,' he observed.

'Yes,' she agreed. 'I do a lot of travelling. He is a homemaker.'

PC Broadbent asked Mr Mollo a few questions, then thanked him for his assistance and put the phone down.

'A flash of blue light,' he recapped. 'Or, as your husband put it, a big blue flesh. Any problems in the marriage?'

'At this moment, yes,' said Mrs Mollo. 'Our children are in the custody of aliens.'

'Can you describe them?'

'Rosi is four years old and beautiful, with blonde hair like the fleece of a sheep. Irmin is two and a half years old and not so beautiful, quite average I would say, with a round face and short hair like a mouse. A sort of greyish-brown. Brownish-grey.'

'I meant the aliens, actually.'

'Very short and... stocky. Like Italians. Italians from the south, not the north. Peasant Italians.'

'I've never been to Italy,' said Broadbent. 'The wife is always at me to go.'

'It's worth the trouble, overall,' said Mrs Mollo. 'Now, are you going to help me?'

✕

It was midsummer, so dawn was underway by the time Frau Mollo and the female police officer arrived at Wombwell Woods. The car park at the Woodhead Lane entrance was deserted. The two women – both approximately the same height, age and build – got out of the police vehicle and continued on foot. WPC Duffy did not advance with a gun held steady in her upraised hand, or with her shoulders hunched in readiness for combat. She walked in a leisurely fashion, keeping her eyes on the path ahead, alert not for clues but for dog turds. The sunrise was elegant and the scenery well-designed. There were thickets of attractively speckled trees, stretches of pure blue water, discreet signs imploring people not to litter, and colourful strews of garbage. All the usual features of a semi-natural municipal green space, except for the nature-loving citizens and their dogs, who were still asleep in the town.

'Where now?' said WPC Duffy.

'It was a picnic area, I think.'

As they walked, Constable Duffy brought her counselling skills into play.

'The pressures of daily life can sometimes push us to make impulsive decisions,' she remarked. 'It all gets too much.'

'I'm sorry to hear that,' said Mrs Mollo. 'I hope I will not keep you too long on this search. But it was pitch-dark when I arrived and everything looks different now.'

'Yes, things can look very different in the clear light of day,' said WPC Duffy, doing her best to inject each word with extra philosophical nuance.

'Like those trees,' said Mrs Mollo. 'I thought there were thousands of them, with no space in between. They're really quite sparse.'

They pressed on. A large bird flew overhead, which made the German woman flinch. WPC Duffy decided that a less allusive, more direct approach might work best.

'Have you ever thought of running away from your husband?'

Mrs Mollo ignored the question. 'I think it was a little further over there.'

'Just taking the children and... disappearing?'

'Wennigsen has a very good school. Rosi is happy there and I'm sure that when the time comes, Irmin will be treated with the patience he needs.' Mrs Mollo swallowed hard and her eyes glimmered.

'It's quite common for a woman to be persuaded to join her lover in another country,' suggested Constable Duffy gently, 'only to find out when she gets there that he's married. And perhaps even a criminal. You'd be surprised how often that happens.'

'We turn left here, I think.'

'Sex is a powerful motivation for all of us.'

'I recognise those wooden tables.'

They walked into the clearing designated for picnics. The benches and tables, constructed of simple planks bolted together, glowed like Stonehenge in the dawn light. The ground, an expanse of grass – almost lawn – was dotted with dandelions. It was also freshly scorched with a huge, circular brand where the green grass had turned black.

Mrs Mollo stepped inside the ring and positioned herself in the centre. She looked up at the empty sky.

'You must help me,' she said. 'You cannot help me.'

Constable Duffy produced her police notebook, checked the exact time, and wrote a few lines. She was ready to ask some more questions now; different questions. She squinted into the brilliance of the rising sun as the silhouette of a woman swayed from side to side.

'We can arrange to get you back home. To Germany. Probably,' she said.

But Mrs Mollo was lost in her own world.

# KINDRED

### *by* JACKIE KAY

**B**EING DEAD IS not at all like I imagined when I was a kid. I imagined the dead would be pale and quiet, and that if they walked at all, they'd walk like zombies, in shuffling slippers, and if they talked at all, they'd whisper and have gravelly rasping voices like the voice of what's his face in *Oliver*, the guy that teaches them all to steal. It's gone. Not the Artful Dodger and not Bill Sykes, but... never mind. It's not the end of the world forgetting bits and pieces, but when I was alive I was a mine of information. People used to say that to me: Martha, you're a mine of information. Much sought after, me, for the pub quiz! And now that I'm dead, I'm still being headhunted which is kind of funny. People come to me to ask loaded questions. Things like: how long will it be before I disintegrate? How long before I start to smell really bad? How long before I get to contact my family? I tell it like it is; I say, you're already disintegrated, mate, and you are a bit whiffy, darling, and you don't get to contact your family, but they can get in touch with you, if they make a little effort, sweetheart. (We dead do have a weakness for those terms of endearment.) What we've got in this *Elsewhere* is not mind, body and spirit, but double spirit and a bit of mind. The body's gone; some people arrived with bits missing anyway, or bits that were supposed to be revamped that never quite worked like the original. You can't really beat the original leg or kidney, it's got to be said.

You go to *Limbo* first and then you come on here, to *Elsewhere*. It's quite a classy joint because there's an air of sophistication to the place. In *Limbo*, there's a scrabbling, squabbling thing going on: people complaining, saying *it's not fair, why me, I wasn't ready, I was robbed, I was snatched away, I was in my prime...* and a whole load of other clichés. In *Limbo*, everything you hear you've heard before. I felt myself getting impatient. I said to a newly-arrived one day, 'Look, you're dead, get over yourself.' which might seem a bit harsh, but once we both turned up in *Elsewhere*, she came up to me and said 'Thanks.' Thanks! 'That was the best piece of advice anyone's ever given me.' It was lovely, that. Such a simple thing – thanks. We dead thrive on thanks; it keeps the spirit elevated.

What we've all got in common here is that no one really deserves to die and all of us have died in different ways. I'll tell you how I died when I've got to know you better. We're like prisoners in that respect; we don't just blurt out intimate details about our death in the first ten minutes. We wait; we take our time to

tell our sad tales. (Few of us claim to have had a *good death* –
what an oxymoron that! – though some are heartened at having
had the chance to say goodbye.) Everyone has a unique story in
some ways because all deaths are unique, at least to the one that
died. But in other ways, every death resembles another and many
common factors are involved: the heart stops beating, the blood
stops pumping, the lungs stop taking in air, the skin stops breath-
ing... These things unite us all. But we've a lot else in common
too because I'm telling you: *death is a great leveller*. Don't matter
if you were rich or if you were poor, if you were black or white,
if you were clever or stupid, once you end up in *Elsewhere* you
are all DEAD. There's more equality here than I could ever have
dreamed of! It's quite touching! And another strange thing: there's
a better quality of conversation because nobody, NOBODY, is
interested in material things. The reason we aren't interested in
material things is because we aren't material. I'm not trying to
be smart, just telling it like it is. But beyond that, we've become
a whole lot more philosophical now that we are dead. We weigh
things up differently and things that used to matter a lot – a new
pair of trainers, a new mobile phone, an iPad, BlackBerry, Xbox,
detox, botox, Sky box, highlights in the hair, extensions to the
house – are all meaningless here. In fact, we look back at our
former selves and wonder how we could ever have cared about
these things. It's fascinating how grotesque the whole of the twen-
tieth century becomes from the pure and clean vantage point of
the dead. Our old obsessions are not so much shaming, because
we have no shame, as puzzling. Most peculiar: did we really care
about THAT?

The other thing that's been VERY interesting is that those that were celebrities when alive aren't famous dead. I remember a pop star turning up one day, and expecting us all to be dead impressed and thinking that somehow there would be an RIP room or something; that you'd be able to sign up for a kind of *deluxe* death; use your former fame to get the real VIP treatment. I went over and spoke to her. I said quietly, we have none of that here. There is no special treatment. We are all the same. We are all just dead people. If she had had eyes, they would have widened. But she didn't have eyes. Her spirit shuffled and blew and shrugged, and eventually settled. And she too came later, and thanked me, and said that nobody had ever talked to her like that in her life. And I said to her, quick as a dead person – because that's another fallacy: the dead aren't slow, they are fast – I said to her 'That's another lovely thing about being dead. There's no bullshit. Nobody tells lies to you like they lied to us living.' I felt the warm air of her accord.

So much is different here to what I imagined. I thought I would do nothing with my time except look down. I always visualised death: high in the sky, all the better to see my loved ones down below and clock what they were up to, perhaps a bit frustrated that I could no longer communicate directly with them. But in actual fact, I'm too busy with stuff going on here, I'm needed in other ways, so I only get to check in with my live friends every so often, once in a blue moon. (And we do get blue moons here; they're extraordinarily beautiful.) In any case, the dead need me more than the living. My whole family's expanded. It's weird but I've seen that family's got nothing to do with genes and blood and DNA: it's got to do with feeling and pluck and loyalty. The old nuclear family is such a small and selfish unit really, compared to what we've got going on here. Seriously – the dead are so much more well-connected. And we've got the time to see how it works: it is not six degrees of separation; when you are dead – two degrees, max. It takes seconds to trace one person to another, to connect them; and of course, here, we discover links to people that were hidden from us in life. Yesterday, a mother and daughter met for the first time. The mother had given the daughter up for adoption when she was seventeen. It was quite touching, but also sobering, because although they greeted each other and were clearly pleased, their spirits bobbing a bit, they didn't really see it as the be-all and end-all, because all the being and seeing had ended. A new thing had begun; they were just as interested in meeting others that weren't related. To put it simply: when you've no longer got any blood, how interested in blood can you be? You get my drift? It's amazing! Everything shifts and changes perspective here in *Elsewhere*.

I know – of course I do – that it's perhaps a bit odd being an enthusiast for death. It might even seem like a contradiction in terms: *an enthusiastic dead person, hello?* Or, it might seem disingenuous, or worse, some kind of con-trick. But it is none of those. It's not like I'm attempting to persuade any of the living to come on over to my place. Not at all! Nor am I trying to do a kind of hard sell for death. That would be pointless since you all must know, even those in denial, that death will surely come for you one day. No, but what I am trying to do, and I will admit to this, is change our image. We must be the most maligned, the most trashed, the most disadvantaged group ever. People say ill-informed and stereotypical things about us every day, ad nausea, ad infinitum. We get to hear! We're not deaf, us dead. We are not resting. We are not at peace. We have not fallen asleep. We are not silent. We are not ghosts, or ghouls, or full of envy for the living. We are neither vengeful nor maladjusted. We are not bitter or twisted. We did not lose our fight or our battle. Actually, it might surprise you to know that we are, much to our own surprise, having a whale of a time. We've met up with so many old friends, and quickly made new ones, and we've participated in rigorous and scintillating conversations. We haven't had to shop, to cook, to wash a dish, to worry about what to eat, what to wear, where to go, what to say, or to clock in or out for ages. We haven't had to be afraid of love. We're a disparate bunch; we've all got different ways of dealing with being dead, but on the whole I think we are a lot more likeable than the living. You see the dead have no ambition. What a relief that is! The dead have no competitions. The dead don't really care what you think except what you think about being dead. We care about *that* because it's hurtful that so many people get us wrong so much of the time. And it is not only hurtful, it's irritating.

Let me tell you a single story. Let me take one recent story and let it stand for all of us. And if this story gets through to you, I promise you that you will see all of us differently, all of us who roam the rugged, peaty hills and glens of *Elsewhere*. A girl arrived in *Limbo*, dead on arrival, like we all do and did, when the moon was full in the sky and the stars were closely making their constellations – here we call them consolations, because the stars console. She had been killed by a hit and run driver and she was ten years old. When someone arrives in *Limbo*, we in *Elsewhere* get sent updates; especially if they think somebody will need extra help here. Two days after Genevieve arrived, her mother followed. She'd been a single mum of a single daughter and she just wanted to be with Genevieve. At first Genevieve was a little stand-offish with her mother. But then the two of them got on famously and made many extra friends, became here in *Elsewhere* part of our huge family. Genevieve's mum who is called Jane, 'just plain Jane,' she said when she arrived, is one of the most generous spirits I've ever met.

It reminded me, because I confess that it often escapes my mind, of myself. There are cycles and cycles when I just don't think about how I got here. It's not what is important anymore. My life was important, and now my death-life is important, but the day I died I would always rather forget. Some time after Jane arrived we had a long conversation. Jane said that she had always thought that if anything happened to her daughter she wouldn't be able to survive. So the taking of her own life wasn't something she agonised over; it was automatic, it was quick, it was a relief. It wasn't so automatic for me, I told her. I was ill for a long time. I tried often and didn't succeed. I kept being brought back to life, and every time I was brought back I resented it. I felt useless. I said to myself, back then, you can't even succeed in killing yourself. You can't even get *that* right. I wasn't crying for help. I really didn't want to be saved and then saved again. 'You must have wanted to be saved,' Jane said. 'You must have or you wouldn't have been. It's that simple.' I went to argue with her when I had a flash of realisation. I *had* wanted to live; and then all of a sudden

I *had* wanted to die. I knew that the people I left behind might think all sorts about me: that I was selfish, a coward, a shirker of responsibility, monstrous, atheist. But I was somebody who, on the night I took my life, could really not stand a second longer. I was as down as I could ever have been.

So imagine my surprise when I came here and literally transformed overnight! I went from somebody who suffered from depression to an optimist. I changed from somebody who didn't enjoy thinking to a real thinker. It's true to say that I am so much happier dead than alive. And the other weird thing is that the people who are like me and Jane are amongst the happiest here in *Elsewhere* and the quickest to adjust, quicker than the ones that have been killed on the spot, and happier even than the ones who have had long and protracted illnesses.

Amongst the maligned dead, those of us who have committed suicide are perhaps the most maligned. The thing I've noticed we all have in common is that we wish we had managed to leave without leaving behind so much guilt. The guilt of the living can weigh heavily on us dead, until we find ways to shake it off, like birds shaking off their many feathers. Which is to say that we don't; we realise we need our feathers in order to fly. Like I said before, the thinking of the dead is quite complicated; we happily turn double negatives into positives.

Today, I took a look in on my daughter; she was nineteen when I took my life. She is now forty-five. I saw her in bed with another woman and she laughed my old laugh and looked the happiest I'd seen her look in years. I made something happen in her room and I saw her look surprised and as if she was looking for me, as I've seen her do so often over the years when I've managed to leave the odd little gift of a red robin or a heron or a whole icicle inside a window, or a goose feather, or a double rainbow, or some lovely lavish early light on a field of corn rigs – I saw her hesitate and then smile, a wide smile like the one I had with my mouth, and at last, I felt complete. I realised then, too, that I'd been kidding myself on a bit. I'd underestimated the ties that I still had to the living. I'd gone dead independent. But I realised today that the strongest and most lovely feeling to be had amongst the *Elsewhere* spirits is a sense of being here and there, inside and outside, in the world and in the ether world, simultaneously. To feel like you can take part, but that you don't have to, to enjoy the lovely whoosh of crossing the border when you check in on old relatives living relatively well, is one of the finest feelings you can get here. And given we are all, like I said, mind and spirit and no body, these feelings are the equivalent of an excellent meal for us, some jellied eels, pie and mash or mince and potatoes, depending on what you loved and what you remember of what you loved back in the days long gone by.

I will tell you what this place looks like so you have no need of terror. We have such a strong sense of colour, we dead: the magnificence of light, the breath-taking glorious pink sunsets, the sweet comfort of the dark, the fragile soft dawn. There's so much to appreciate and enjoy. And strangely, even the feeling of missing a beloved has something quite kind about it because we dead know the truth: we are loved more than the living! Our faults are forgotten and we are elevated in our death. Even neighbours, when asked about us, if we have been murdered, say lovely things.

Even when we've been a bit of a pain, they'll say, 'He was a really nice guy, kept himself to himself.' Or 'We used to see her taking her kids to school; she always had a hello for everybody.' But, of course, flattery gets the dead nowhere! We are not asking for much really, except that the living should broaden their minds, should think as positively about the state we are in as they do about individual qualities we might once have had. If there's one thing I've learnt here in *Elsewhere* it is that money matters not one jot and that life and death have more in common than you might think. I could go on. I could go on and on. That's one difference, I guess. The dead can go on and on and on. At some point the living have to stop.

# VANISHING POINT

## *by* LOUISE WELSH

F ROM THIS POSITION I can see the slow progress of late afternoon shadow across the wall at the end of my bed. When the
shade creeps beyond the top corner, turning it from stark white to a
pale shade of blue-grey, someone will come and turn me. Then I'll
see the bottom of the door, the scuffed legs of the visitor's chair, the
grey vinyl floor occasionally enlivened by a tuft of stoor. I prefer the
top corner, the unstoppable march of shadow played out each day
across the intersection of edge and wall, my vanishing point.

In the morning when my mother visits, neon tubes turn the
room a startling sugar-cube bright. I'm clean and freshly wiped.
Mother kisses my cheek, strokes the hair back from my face, and
tells me about her world. A scream used to form in my head as
her voice trembled through news of names I hardly knew, but the

wall has taught me patience. The tides of words lose themselves of meaning, reduced to a rhythm that sings of my childhood.

I stare at the corner. It's clean and neatly defined. A meeting of boundaries composed of three lines. Both walls and ceiling end in right angles, but their union bestows a triangular aspect, like the crease of leg and lap that meet at the top of a woman's thighs.

Once she's brought me up to date my mother opens her bag and takes out a book. Apart from the moment when I'm rolled from the view of floor and stoor to the crispness of angles, this is the highlight of my day.

When I was first locked in Mother used to follow news of her world with news of the world beyond. The newspaper would be unfurled and I'd hear the pages rustle as she scanned them for stories fit to repeat. The sessions grew so short she was compelled to read the sports reports.

Then one day a book appeared. She held it in front of my face, blocking my view of the corner, so I could inspect its cover. A vapid blue sky turned to star spattered black as a spaceship hurtled upwards. I wondered if the strain of being boxed in with me each day had turned Mother's mind. But she explained she'd found three boxes of paperbacks abandoned on the pavement outside her building and had paid the grandson of her downstairs neighbour a pound and a volume of his choosing to carry them up to her flat.

The paperbacks' broken spines and well-thumbed pages made it clear they'd been read more than once. Mother had never been attracted to sci-fi before, but she reckoned that books so thoroughly studied must be worth taking a chance on. I don't know if their origins intrigued her from the first, but pretty soon the books became more than their contents to her.

As she reads she explores the pages for clues of where PB Bridgestock (the name is scrawled on the inside cover of each volume) read them before us.

'Look,' she'll say, 'he either dropped this in the bath or sat with it in the steam room for too long. See how the pages are warped? Paper can't take moisture, especially cheap paper like this.' She delights in PB Bridgestock's travels as if they're her own. 'He read this on a beach somewhere. I thought that stain might be hamburger grease, but see, some sand's got into the spine. The mark must be suntan lotion.' And she pauses for a moment as if remembering a world where there are beaches and a sun people oil up for. The books kept PB Bridgestock company at mealtimes (he was a fan of English mustard), on buses and trains, even once or twice on an aeroplane (PB was inclined to use tickets and boarding passes as bookmarks). They had accompanied their original owner on idle afternoons lazing outdoors where tiny insects were inadvertently trapped, then mummified between the pages.

The clues to PB Bridgestock's reading habits that thrill my mother exasperate me. I love the books for their power to lift me up, beyond even the corner. Mother's voice recedes. My crew and I are floating through the universe, on a spacecraft that has lost its bearings in time, certain that somewhere on the ship lies a hostile force. Mother reads on, speeding me through starry galaxies where survival is uncertain and adventures guaranteed.

When it's time for her to leave, I look into Mother's eyes and tell her,

| 9 | 12 | 15 | 22 | 5 | 25 | 15 | 21 |
|---|----|----|----|---|----|----|----|
| I | L | O | V | E | Y | O | U |

Sometimes I say,

| 19 | 15 | 18 | 18 | 25 |
|----|----|----|----|----|
| S | O | R | R | Y |

No one else ever visits, and for that I'm grateful, though some-times I hear old voices, faint, like whispers in a stairwell, *no change, poor soul.*

The doctors do their rounds every afternoon, a recurring drill of charts and low exchanges with the duty nurse. They generally leave without acknowledging me. But occasionally one or other of them will take the time to sit by my bed and ask how I am. I say,

| 16 | 12 | 5 | 1 | 19 | 5 |
|----|----|---|---|----|---|
| P | L | E | A | S | E |

| 11 | 9 | 12 | 12 | 13 | 5 |
|----|---|----|----|----|---|
| K | I | L | L | M | E |

The doctors know how much the *please* cost me, fifty-eight flick-ers of my eyes.

Late afternoon drifts into dusk as my mother switches from one bus to another and then another. One of PB Bridgestock's books is tucked safe in her bag and she stares out of the window at drivers stalled in the tailbacks that line her route. Some sing or smoke or talk lawlessly on mobiles, but mostly they sit alone, their faces unreadable.

Sometimes a stranger sits next to her and begins a conversation. She rouses herself knowing that, at her age, politeness depends on cheer.

'I was just in town picking up a bit of shopping,' she usually says, though sometimes her inventions surprise herself; grandchildren who grow out of their shoes as if there's no tomorrow, a husband who demands his steak comes from a far-flung butcher, a meeting of some vague committee she takes the minutes for. From time to time she'll say, 'I was up at the hospital, visiting my daughter.'

My mother unlocks the door to her apartment. She sets her bags in the kitchen, slips off her shoes and then walks barefoot through to the bedroom where she changes into her house clothes. The neat-made bed tempts her, but sleep is an enemy and a nap now will almost certainly mean a wakeful night. She pulls on her slippers and returns to the kitchen where she unpacks her messages before sitting at the kitchen table and lighting up a cigarette. Mother sits smoking by the open window, feeling the night air on her skin, looking out at the apartment blocks beyond, each one a perfect mirror of the block that contains her.

I look at the sure stillness of the corner and imagine myself made small, sitting in the cockpit of a rocket, speeding towards it. The corner spins open, a portal admitting me to its whiteness. I pull down on the joystick and zoom on, into the blackness beyond. The hospital buildings shine palely below, tiny in the dark, the H of the helipad smaller than the nail on my pinky. The rocket zooms on, along the route it took my mother hours to travel and within seconds I'm hovering bright and silent outside her kitchen. She gets to her feet stubbing out the cigarette, opening the window wide. The rocket sweeps into the brightness of the room, and I see the same table, the same lino, the same wallpaper I knew as a child. The past is real and everything beyond it a dream.

I lower the door of the rocket and mother climbs its ramp. She smiles as she buckles in, our eyes meet and all of a sudden we're laughing. I fire up the engines and we speed out through the window, vanishing into the beyond, bound for elsewhere.

# SOUTH

## *by* GILLIAN PHILIP

I<small>CE LIES IN</small> a thin slick across the bay, but he's in the water anyway. The boy always is. Just like his grandmother.

It might as well be the other side of the earth: her side of it. A late and overcast day in monochrome, showing only white, and spikes of grass and tree, and the hills drawn in charcoal streaks with scribbles of gully in between. Not so much snow, now.

The world's only colour lies in the beam of the Land Rover headlights – sick yellow of winter grass, a few dull pink yards of road. I switch off the engine and the lights too. Creak the door open into silence, and walk down to the shore, tightening my scarf round my neck. Cold burns my throat when I call to him.

'Culley. Time to come home now.'

I wait, used to it now, the tight slow thump of my heart as I wait for him to not-come-back. One day he'll be gone. One day, like his mother.

Not today.

He hauls himself from the water, nostrils flaring open, cropped hair stiff with salt against his long skull, bits of ice still glittering in it. He towels his scalp with one hand, pulls on jeans with the other, tugging denim over damp skin.

He smiles at me. 'Grandpappy.'

'Culley. Your father is worried. It's late.'

He looks at the sky, surprised. 'I was just coming.'

Like a boy hauled from the slides in the play park, he's sheep-ish, apologetic, a little resentful.

The relief chokes my throat, so to pass the embarrassing moment I bend to retrieve his jumper from the black rocks, and hand it to him. Unhurried, he pulls it over his head; big as it is, it stretches across his overdeveloped shoulders. He smiles at me again, his dark hair stiff with salt and frost but already drying.

'I'll take you back,' I say.

'Thanks. I'm sorry. It's hard to know the time.' He scratches his scalp nervously, and the frost-light makes the slight membrane between his fingers look thinner than ever.

He's a gentle boy. He doesn't like to cause hurt, regrets it when he so often does. I don't worry for him. Not much.

I keep the rifle in the Land Rover, but I know I won't need it.

✕

His grandmother looked much the same, first time I saw her.

Half-naked, that is, not gentle. In that climate I thought she was mad, with nothing but a silky-fur blanket clasped round her like a cloak.

I'd gone to watch the penguins because I had some time off, and watching the penguins was a hobby for me, not work like it was for Mal. He watched penguins and fur seals and sometimes leopard seals, when there were any, when there was ice in the bay. They didn't come in the warmer weather. He watched them and counted them and made records, and because those were the days before the internet, he sent data back home on the Inmarsat. I helped him, when I wasn't fixing things. He loved his job, and I loved mine. You had to, or you wouldn't be out on this lonely outcrop of a godforsaken island.

The unexpected woman sat on a rock, watching the penguins too, and they seemed more nervous of her than of me, but I wasn't watching emperors any more. I laid my binoculars down because I didn't need them; she was that close.

When they say blood runs cold it's a cliché, but there's no other way to describe it. She wasn't supposed to be there. I'd thought Mal and I were alone at this end of the island, and I thought for a ridiculous moment she'd missed her cruise ship and been left behind. Except that people off the cruise ships didn't dress like that – half-naked under a silky-fur wrap.

She turned her head and looked at me.

'Are you all right?' I asked.

My gut had tightened with the fear of madness. It was well below zero but her pale skin didn't prickle with gooseflesh and she didn't shiver, not once. Her hair was sleek and black and wet, and for a crazy moment I thought she must have been in the water. But that wasn't possible. Not in her skin.

'I'm fine,' she smiled, 'I'm grand. Hello yourself.'

To step away from a near-naked woman, and one so beautiful: that would have been the mad thing. And when Malcolm found out, as he certainly would the next time we got garrulous with homesickness and rum, he'd never let me forget it.

So I took a step closer instead, and saw that her hair wasn't black at all but an odd iron-grey, with a hint of what might have been dappling. And though she was so tall and straight and slender, and her face was a long reptilian oval – which isn't to say it wasn't beautiful – her shoulders looked disproportionately powerful. She smelt of the sea: of grease-ice and salt and tussac grass, and quite possibly penguin-shit. I fell in love.

I said, 'You'll have to come back to the base. You'll have to come back with me.'

×

I'm a practical man. I'm not a scientist like Mal but an engineer. I fix things. I fix plumbing and generators and wireless masts and chemical toilets, when they need fixing. So I'm practical, and I'm rational, but where I come from they do have the seal stories. I thought the superstitions and the myths and the legends all came from the same place I did. It never occurred to me there could be others. I didn't know there'd be an equivalence, a balance in the round globe, a mirror image of the north, if you like, which was the south.

I thought they made the seal stories because common seals look so human: gentle and intelligent and empathetic. But those seals of the south don't look human. Or if they do, it's another kind of human altogether.

I should have thought. But I didn't think. I didn't think at all in the months, turning into years, when Elin was mine.

✕

Mal counted the leopard seals and studied them, and he loved them and respected them, but he feared them properly too. He stayed out of the water when the ice was in the bay, and he stayed away from the land's edge when the penguins flocked like a black-and-white buffet. He didn't want to be mistaken for one, he said, laughing.

Elin liked Mal. She laughed when he laughed, but I was never jealous. It never occurred to me that she'd be unfaithful; she was too possessive, too passionate for that. She didn't want to go back, she said, to the small fishing settlement on the other side of the island. She liked scientists, that's why she'd come. She liked engineers too, and me best of all.

She got pregnant, of course. I hadn't exactly thought to stock up on supplies that might prevent that. I wanted her to leave the island then, to come with me on the red-hulled supply ship when it next called. She refused.

Unnervingly, she refused any help at all. The pregnancy couldn't have been as long as it seemed; I must have lost count of the months. She was restless and discontented, and liked to be alone, and one day she didn't come back for all my searching and screaming, or Mal's. She simply reappeared the next day with her infant.

She smiled, her dappled hair plastered to her head, but the dampness wasn't sweat, because when I kissed it and kissed it, holding onto her fiercely, it smelt of seawater, and ice, and penguin-shit, and blood.

I loved our baby so ferociously, fear settled into me and wouldn't leave. Children change things. Not outwardly, though; not for a while. I was too embarrassed to confide my suspicions to Mal, and I didn't want to argue with Elin, so as usual we'd sit in the evenings, all three of us – four, with our quiet, ravenous daughter – and we drank rum and talked and laughed and spoke about the fur seals and the supply ship and the weather coming in across the razor-edged hills.

Elin got along great with Mal, but nobody stays on the base forever; nobody, it seemed, except her. And now me, and our child. Mal's replacement, when he chose to leave, was a spiky little man called Thewlis. I didn't especially want a replacement for Mal, but then the base didn't belong to me or the others who came through. The base wasn't Elin's. A replacement for Mal had to come to count the penguins and the fur seals, to record them and measure them and send the data back.

Thewlis respected the leopard seals as much as Mal did. He'd get out of the water if there was one there with him. They weren't aggressive, only curious, but you never knew. You never knew, and you could only remember Shackleton's wild stories, and take account of anecdote and an earlier, less scientific age.

Thewlis understood a lot less about children than about sub-Antarctic fauna, but that was hardly his fault. He simply couldn't understand us keeping Sylvie in the wilderness. We beggared his belief, he said, when he got to know us better. It was mad, bringing up a child here. And soon she'd be of an age for school, and the nearest school was two islands away, and then what were we planning to do?

I hadn't planned anything, but I didn't like to admit that because I'd sound downright gormless.

Thewlis didn't like or understand Sylvie, but that didn't stop him worrying about her. She needed proper paediatric care and a decent education. He wanted us to take her away.

That's not quite true. I was useful; I knew the base and its innards. He wanted Elin to take Sylvie away.

It's not right, he'd say, stroking his little beard, all concerned. It's no environment for a youngster.

Elin said that Sylvie ruined the environment for him; that was his trouble.

'I think it's only right,' he told me quietly, one evening after he finally browbeat me into agreement, the evening before the red-hulled ship was due to dock again and take us north to civilisation and nursery school and paediatricians. 'The older she gets, the more she'll need to be away from here.'

I knew he wanted the bleak beauty of the place to be child-free, but I also knew he was right. So I drank too much, and Elin stormed out in a temper, pulling her fur wrap around her winter clothes and slamming the door. She must have expected to be very cold. Indeed, she was gone all night and between alcohol and anxiety I didn't sleep at all. I turned over and stared into the dark and worried till the palest streak of dawn let me get up.

Stiff and bleary, I opened the blind. There was ice in the bay.

I saw Thewlis close to the base; he'd only just set out on his rounds of the ragged shoreline. He glanced up at me, waved. I waved back, and thought about the glitch with the generator and how I could fix that one last thing before I left.

I sighed and blinked hard at my headache, and that's why I didn't quite see the lunging shadow. If I saw it at all it was a blur on the edge of my vision, like a fleeting, flaring cataract.

I heard his hoarse howl, and then I was running, grabbing my boots on, not bothering with my anorak. I hoped Thewlis could keep his hold on the frayed edge of the ice, because he wouldn't live if he went in the water, not when something had pulled him there like a striking snake.

I thought I ran fast, but by the time I reached the brink of the land, scattering offended penguins, there was nothing on the ice but a smear of blood.

We found Thewlis later that day: me, two fishers, and my own replacement plus the supply ship's crew after it docked. We hunted for hours, and I thought we might not see him again at all. One of the fishers from the little town brought a pistol; it was too late for that, but I didn't say so.

When we found his sodden corpse, Thewlis was barely touched; I thought he might even be alive, till we rolled him over and saw his skull, crushed by a single bite.

When we told Sylvie she ran sobbing in shock to her mother, who stood soberly at the base door and wrapped the girl in her arms and kissed her dappled hair.

✕

Later, the two of us argued so badly that the others left us alone to it, going outside to try to smoke in air that was minus ten and falling.

'It was a leopard seal,' I yelled at Elin. 'I'm not changing our plans. We'll still take Sylvie when the ship leaves. It's dangerous here.'

'It isn't dangerous for *her*,' she spat. 'Thewlis antagonised it. He must have.'

'You're being selfish,' I shouted. 'Because you don't want to leave.'

'And neither does she. And she never will.'

And of course she flew out again, slamming the door so hard it bounced. I rolled my eyes. Her rage was too much of a habit for me to care. Instead of caring I drank more, and laughed with the crew and the new engineer and the men from the settlement, and drank even more. Sylvie played quietly in the corner of the room with her plastic Sea Life animals, and looked morosely, but only occasionally, towards the door.

I drank beyond the point of not caring, to a state of suddenly caring very desperately. I was drunk and maudlin and angry, so when I stood up fast, I knocked over the chair.

I blinked, and stared at the abandoned Sea Life set. 'Where's Sylvie?'

✕

Sylvie wasn't far away. I saw her in the light of stars and ice: ice in the bay, ice on the edge of land and life. The child was laughing, dangling her bare feet into freezing water, leaning down to the sleek raptor head raised above the greasy slick of ice.

'No,' I screamed. 'No.'

It bared dinosaur teeth as ancient as death. Sylvie hesitated, looked back at me, then at the seal. I was drowning its growls with my furious frightened yells, and I was outpacing the men behind me. I'd scared her. Sylvie began to cry.

'Daddy,' she wailed.

As I hurtled towards her I saw that blurred shadow lunge again, and the seal had her leg.

And I had her arm, but only just. I looked at the seal and I knew it would tear her in half sooner than let her go. It glared hatred, my daughter's blood on its teeth, and suddenly I wasn't drunk any more. I wasn't drunk when I yelled 'Shoot it! Shoot it!' and the man running up behind me fired a shot into the sleek reptilian head.

But my vision was blurred all the same, and my eyes stung with awful grief, and the head was sliding under the surface, wolf-eyes turning dull, full of hatred, then full of nothing but death, and then lost in the deep cold water, trailing a single tendril of blood.

✕

I took Sylvie home. I didn't love the island any more. My daughter had health checks and hospital treatment and an education, but she walked with a limp ever after, a limp and a faraway sadness. She limped down the aisle on her wedding day, and she limped to the boy Culley's baptism, and I daresay she limped the day she went to the sea at last and didn't come back.

On that day and many days after, Culley's father howled with grief, so I got him drunk and patted his shoulder, but I knew I shouldn't cry myself because, after all, I'd cheated the sea of her for long enough.

And I did have Sylvie's son, because she was better than her mother. She was just selfish enough to go to the sea, but not quite selfish enough to take the boy with her.

Still I worry. I go down to the bay that's a mirror reflection of one in the far south, and I shiver in the darkness and count seconds, and wait for Culley to not-come-back.

And sometimes him not-coming-back isn't the worst thing I imagine, when he smiles at me and his canines gleam in moonlight, and his hug is so strong and fierce it could drag me under.

I keep the rifle in the Land Rover.

It's not as if I'll need it.

# ELSEWHERE, FAR FROM HERE

## *by* ALBERTO MANGUEL

*Elsewhere, far from here! Too late! Maybe never!*
—Charles Baudelaire, *A une passante*

ULYSSES TURNED HIS back on the harbour and followed a rough track leading through the woods and up to the hills towards the place where Athena had told him. A group of men were idling around an oil barrel in which a fire was burning. He muttered a greeting and stood for a moment with them, trying to warm his hands. Then he entered the town through a crumbling stone gate.

Athena had wanted to be paid in full before leading him onto the ship, and then the captain had asked for further payment before allowing him and the other four men to crawl into the wooden crate and cover themselves with the raw hides meant for export. The customs people, Athena had told him, hardly ever bothered inspecting a cargo of hides. Afterwards, he'd tried to wash himself off in salt water, but the smell of dead animals still clung to him like a wet cloth.

All the years he'd been away, he'd remembered the way home in snapshots: the house of the Englishwoman, the oak tree inside a ring of stones, the sloping wall which he and his friends used to climb, pretending it was a mountain. Now he let his legs carry him, like mules that knew the way. Straight on, then left, then right, then left again. He looked about in wonder.

Was this the place? Were these the houses he knew, built this way and that? Were the shutters painted that colour? From the many places he had seen he carried images that were not his own, and now they overlapped and stuck to the half-remembered sites in a confusion of impressions. As a child, it was all clear-cut: a word for everything around him, a tag for every event, for every person. Not now. Already the harbour looked different: loads of fruit from the Caribbean, tractors from the United States, blond men from Norway and Iceland. Places he knew faraway. Not here.

A scent of benzine filled his nostrils, and a purple-coloured dust blew in the air as it never had blown in his childhood. A pale, young, helmeted man stood in a doorway, gently caressing a gun. A 4x4 roared past him and then turned towards the old cemetery. A black man with salt-white hair, blind in one eye, opened and closed a high window. A woman with snakes in her hair sat on a stone bench, shouting curses to the passers-by. A group of children dressed in smocks were throwing stones at a pack of dogs. Even the dogs looked strange. Who were they, these people who'd never belonged here, whose stories were told elsewhere, in languages he never learned to speak, in places where he'd been a foreigner? He stopped by the fountain where his mother and aunts used to fetch the water before the aid workers built the neighbourhood pump.

The Sibyl of Cumae, two thousand years old, was coming up the street with her shopping basket. He recognized her immediately. Huffing and drooling, gobs of spittle forming at the corners of her mouth like foam on an ancient sea, her face, shrivelled and bristly, framed by her kerchief, as he remembered it from Cumae, where he had gone to ask her a question, her body bent over like one of the small old trees that grew in the harbour. She struggled up the street clutching the folds of her black dress.

'Sibyl! Sibyl!' called the children, and laughed. One of the boys threw a stone at her, not meaning to hit her, as if he just wanted her to say something, to answer back.

He then ran to his friends, laughing but also frightened. Ulysses remembered that his mother had told him that the Sibyl lived far across the water and that, once a year, she caught a little child and drained its blood. This kept her young. Ulysses didn't believe his mother, but when he'd approached her in Cumae he'd still been afraid.

'Sibyl! Sibyl!' Ulysses heard a girl call, taller and older than the other children. She had a mane of curly black hair and firm breasts that showed under her shirt. 'Sibyl, tell me, can you teach me how to do it?' And she laughed louder than the others.

'Shameless!' a woman shouted out at the girl. 'How can you say such things?' And she turned to Ulysses as if to seek his support.

The children laughed again, proud of their leader. But the girl had nothing more to say and ran off, and the children followed.

Instead of turning down the street that almost certainly led to his house, Ulysses followed the Sibyl until she reached the marketplace. This too was not as he remembered it. Now, next to the food stalls, there were sellers of polyester dresses and jeans, radios and electric clocks, Russian shoes, German cutlery and Rumanian china. There was a stall that sold tapes and played music: Aldo Freni, Ben Trent, Valentino. The Sibyl stopped to buy grapes which she would swallow whole because her teethless gums couldn't burst the skin, and bread whose crust she'd first cut off with a knife she'd brought to be sharpened. In Cumae, Ulysses had seen her throw the crusts to the ravens outside her door before she'd turned back in and not come out again. He'd left without asking his question.

The Sibyl filled her basket and began the long walk back to her house, a small house on the edge of town. The door was very low, barely high enough for a child; the three small windows were shuttered. Outside there was a wooden bench, weathered and warped, set against the wall. There the Sibyl sat, her basket by her side. A canary sang through the shutters. 'Poor innocent little bird!' said a young couple, passing by. 'Locked up in that darkness of hell!'

In Cumae too, the Sibyl had a house very much like this one. Every evening, except in the depth of winter, the Sibyl would sit on the wooden bench and wait. On the Sibyl's street, no boys played soccer in the evenings, no girls played hopscotch. *When she's walking*, Ulysses thought, *she looks alive, funny with age, an ugly doll. But now that she's sitting, she's as if made of wood, like the bench, or of stone, like the grey house.*

Ulysses waited. From the Sibyl's house he could see the whole town stretching out from wall to crumbled wall and beyond, to the harbour from which he'd come, far in the distance, to his house hidden behind a new grey building crowned with a billboard advertising a supermarket. Athena had led him back, but was this the town he'd left? Again he felt lost. The many years of wandering dragged behind him like the wake of a ship, and were now wearily familiar in the suffering they'd brought; he'd grown accustomed to them as one might grow accustomed to the pain of an old wound. Every new port, every new encounter had made him feel alien in a different way and his senses were now attuned to certain expected sights and sounds and smells: the crash of a door slamming in his face, the raised eyebrow of the bureaucrat fingering his passport, the brackish odour of a meal offered by a kind soul through the bars of an detention camp. A man he'd met on one of his attempts had said to him: 'Once an exile, always an exile.'

He had tried to redo his life in many places. In one, he had been kept imprisoned in a cave-like room, like sheep to be fattened and devoured. In another, he had worked and slept in an underground factory, among clattering machinery, surrounded by men and women who had forgotten even their names. In a third, he had been allowed to stay only if he swore to leave again after a certain time and not claim any of the benefits of an ordinary labourer. In a fourth, he had been forced to hide night and day from the immigration police, and if anyone asked he said his name was Nobody. Twice he had become a whore. In the most dreadful place of all, ghost-like souls past all hope whirled about him in howling droves and told him of the terrible things that had happened to them. Officials with bored faces went around taking down their stories and collecting them in cardboard files.

After Cumae, he'd seen the Sibyl in several of those places, staring blankly among those who had lost all memory, huddled among the *sans-papiers*, wandering among the ghostly asylum-seekers. She had appeared in the midst of them all, or had sat to one side, brooding, or had shuffled with the crowd waiting endlessly in queues to fill in forms, furnish documentation, explain, cajole, plead. He'd seen her once, with two other old women, dragged handcuffed onto a plane between armed *gendarmes*: she had said nothing, but the women were sobbing and screaming, and the other passengers had been very upset. Another time, she had stood among the neighbours watching a small African boy being taken from his school to a waiting car, his teacher shouting curses at the abductors. Then too, the Sibyl had remained silent.

The Sibyl now sat on her bench, her basket by her side, as if she had been sitting there since the beginning of the world. Ulysses looked at her and, for the first time, she looked back at him. He imagined what the old woman saw: an old man, in dirty rags, possessing nothing, belonging nowhere. A question had been shaping itself since he'd left home, in the early years of the war, and after his first death, and then after the second, and later towards the end of the fighting and the city's fall, and all throughout the cursed voyage back, after every new marvel and every new terror. His tongue now mouthed it, mumbling. Then he spoke it again, more clearly.

On her bench, the Sibyl lifted her ancient head. Her breast heaved with an asthmatic wheeze, strands of grey hair which had escaped from under her kerchief blew now against her face and stuck to her wet jaw. She lifted a hand to her mouth but didn't touch her lips. She uttered a low moaning sound, between a grunt and a cackle, let out a whistling sigh, and then a shriek so shrill that the people, coming now up her street in an ever-increasing crowd, failed to hear it.

# THE FUTURE ACCORDING TO LUKE

## by JAMES ROBERTSON

L UKE STANDS ALONE was the worst prophet in the history of
the Lakota people. He went into trances and when he came
out of them he would say he'd seen the future. But he hadn't,
because nearly everything he prophesied had taken place days,
months or years before. Even the century before the last one. He
didn't so much see the future as forget the past, then remember
it again as if it were still to happen. This wasn't something his
friends Dean Liboux and Johnny Little Eagle felt they could really
hold against him, but they weren't filled with a lot of confidence
when he made a prediction.

Dean and Johnny had discussed Luke's prophetic failings often
and concluded that the inside of his head was just a trailer full of
junk, with a TV in the corner playing a continuous stream of old

Westerns, cartoons, commercials and documentaries. Hardly any wonder he got confused. Again, they didn't blame him for this. The insides of their own heads weren't so different.

One time, Luke said he'd seen white soldiers tumbling upside down into an Indian village with their hats falling off. This meant a great victory was coming, he explained.

'You mean an old-time village, with tepees and everything?' Dean asked.

'I guess,' Luke said.

'You guess?' Dean said.

Johnny said, 'Didn't Sitting Bull dream something pretty much like that before Little Big Horn?'

Luke didn't even blink. 'Yeah, you're right, he did. Man, how about that?'

Days went by, and weeks, and Luke wasn't around. Then one day Dean saw him again. 'So when is the big victory coming off?' he demanded.

'It already did,' Luke said. 'They opened the new casino, didn't they?'

'The Prairie Wind? What's that got to do with anything?'

'The first Saturday it was open, a bunch of Air Force personnel came over from Ellsworth and lost two thousand dollars at blackjack. Ain't that a victory?'

'I suppose you're going to tell me they took their hats off when they came inside?' Dean said.

'I guess,' Luke said.

'But there ain't no tepees there. They got a 78-bed hotel, but no tepees.'

'They got tepees on the website,' Luke said. 'Check it out. Just like in my vision.'

Dean didn't have a computer. He could hardly think of anyone he knew who did. He could think of quite a few who had electricity and even a land-line, but computers were thin on the ground on the reservation. Luke himself didn't have one, so he must have seen the website some place else. He used to disappear for long periods, and when he showed up again he would make out he'd been living rough in the Badlands, on a quest for visions, but usually somebody would have spotted him in Rapid City or Sioux Falls. Once even in Denver. Maybe he'd looked at the website in Denver.

There was nothing particularly unusual about the way he took off like that: a lot of folks came and went on the reservation, many of them spent time in the cities, and visions of one kind or another weren't uncommon either. Johnny and Dean had had visions themselves. But these days Dean was trying to avoid them. He wasn't smoking weed or eating magic mushrooms, and although he still liked to drink he was sticking to Budweiser. He'd decided drinking vodka or any of those ten per cent malt liquors was the quickest way to death and he didn't want to go there yet.

As for Johnny, well, Dean didn't know what Johnny wanted. He had a girlfriend who had a baby by another man, and he seemed to like her and the kid but he didn't spend much time with them. He preferred hanging out with his male friends, getting drunk. A lot of guys were like that, whether or not they had girlfriends. Life was difficult and drinking made it easier, at least for a while. Maybe that was what Johnny wanted, just for life to be easier. Maybe that was all anybody could want.

Johnny and Dean were good drinking buddies because neither of them was into fighting – each other or anybody else. They tried to stay away from guys they knew who got fighting drunk, because it hurt too much being punched by them and it hurt too much having to accept their apologies when they sobered up. They both liked drinking with Luke, even if he was a shit prophet, because he didn't want to fight either. The three of them would sit around moaning about all the bad things that had already happened to the Lakota, and Luke would foretell all the bad things that were still to come.

Of course you didn't have to be a prophet to be able to do that, you just had to walk around with your eyes and ears open. Luke could tell you, for instance, that in the next three months there would be X number of car wrecks involving Y number of Indians, and you knew that, give or take a few, his prophecy would come true. He could give you similar predictions about how many people on the reservation would die of alcohol poisoning, how many overdose, how many be murdered, how many commit suicide, how many be assaulted, how many be arrested, how many get jobs, how many lose them, how many reach the age of fifty, how many not – until at last, maybe around the fifth or sixth beer, you'd say, 'But Luke, you ain't saying nothing we don't already know.' And Luke would say, 'Yeah, but wasn't I right about the Little Big Horn?' or, 'Wasn't I right about the casino?' And you didn't argue with him, you just laughed, because what else could you do? And anyway, you weren't drinking to argue, you were drinking to get drunk.

Selling, buying or drinking alcohol was illegal on the reservation. So what Dean and Johnny would do was drive over the boundary to Jubal Schele's place, the Buffalo Saloon, and drink there. This one day they had scraped together a few dollars – enough to put some gas in Johnny's beat-up old car – and had set off up the road, and after a few miles they passed Luke Stands Alone walking, so they pulled over and gave him a ride.

It was a cold, clear afternoon in November. When they arrived at the Buffalo Saloon and got out of the car, Dean saw snow on the distant Black Hills. He drew this to the attention of the others. 'Yeah, I dreamed about that,' Luke said. 'I saw it on the weather report,' Johnny said.

The bar was situated on a rough old back route between Bombing Range Road and the highway to Custer, and the only reason for it being there was to serve liquor to Indians. The big old sign on the roof said INDIANS ALLOWED, which kind of proved the point, but the story was that back in the fifties the words NO DOGS OR had also been up there. Dean asked Jubal if this was true. He asked it in a friendly enough way, but Jubal looked at him suspiciously, like he was trying to start some trouble, even though they were the only customers.

'What if it did?' Jubal said. 'That's an artefact, that sign, a piece of the old days.'

'Them old days,' Johnny said sourly. 'Ain't they over, Jubal?'

'They sure are,' Jubal grumbled, in a way that made you understand he missed them. 'Genuine goddamn piece of Old West memorabilia, that sign.'

'Maybe you should try selling it on eBay,' Johnny said.

'Why would I do that?' Jubal said. 'Might want to sell the whole place some day, and that sign's a part of it. Integral, you know? So I think I'll leave it where it is. You boys wanting some more beers now?'

While Jubal was away Johnny said there could be no greater irony than three Lakota men of warrior age drinking liquor in a white man's bar located midway between a town called Custer and a US Air Force bombing range, and Dean said, oh yes there could, those same three Indians could be laughing about it. So they laughed about it and then Jubal came back with the beers and took the money from the pile of dirty dollar bills and quarters in the middle of the table. Jubal was happy for them to drink as much as they liked, but he didn't keep a tab, not for Indians here in the back room. If there were ever any white customers in the front room, maybe tourists headed for Mount Rushmore, he'd have kept a tab for them, but there never were.

Dean went to the men's room to take a leak. The walls were painted a deep brick red that was almost brown, and there were darker, menacing stains in several places. There had been an infamous fight at the Buffalo Saloon once, many years ago, before Dean was even born, between some reservation Indians and some outsiders, city Indians. Skins versus breeds. The fight had been in the bar and then somebody had followed somebody else out to the men's room, and a gun had been pulled, and a man had been shot and killed. Just thinking about it spooked Dean a little. He seemed to recall that the man hadn't died right there, but later, in hospital. For a while after that the Buffalo Saloon had had a bad reputation and was always busy. That was when Jubal should have sold the joint. These days it was mostly quiet. There were other places just off the reservation that you could walk to, and where you could get drunk for less – liquor stores, not bars. They were the places most people went to now.

For all that he didn't want to fight, Dean kind of wished he'd been at Jubal's back then. He wished something would happen. It wouldn't matter if it was good or bad. Just if something would happen. He felt like he wasn't fully alive, like somebody had reached in and taken some vital organ out of his body while he was sleeping. It was weird: he couldn't remember ever not feeling like that, but he'd only recognised it in the last year. Somebody had stolen something from him, his ability to get angry or even just active. Maybe it was to do with drinking too much. Or maybe, now that he was cutting down, it was to do with not drinking enough. Hell, he was only twenty-five, maybe he'd stop altogether. If he did, would the feeling be there all the time, or would it go away forever?

Back in the bar, Luke had started to tell Johnny his latest prophecy. 'You got to hear this,' Johnny said. 'Start again, Luke.' So Luke started again.

'I had a vision about you guys,' he said. 'The two of you. Only I couldn't tell which one of you was which.'

'I'm Johnny,' said Dean quickly, just as Johnny said, 'I'm Dean.'

'In the vision,' Luke said. 'I couldn't tell in the vision. Do you want to hear it or not?'

They wanted to hear it.

'You're standing on a road. A straight road heading right across the prairie. And a pick-up comes by and pulls over. The driver is a big white man. He's wearing a white hat and there's a rifle slung along the back of the cab. He offers one of you a ride, I don't know which, and I'm saying, no, no, don't get in.'

'What were you doing there?' Dean asked.

'I was there but I kind of wasn't, know what I mean? And I'm shouting at you not to get in the pick-up but you don't hear me.'

'So do I get in?' Johnny said.

'What about me?' Dean said. 'Do I?' Because they still weren't taking Luke seriously.

'Neither of you gets in. First he offers you a ride. Then he offers you a blanket. I'm shouting, don't take the blanket, it's full of smallpox. Then he offers you a bottle of whisky. I'm shouting, don't take the whisky, it'll poison you.'

'And what are we doing, just standing around while this guy offers us things?' Johnny said.

'Pretty much. It's like I said, I couldn't see which one of you he was talking to. The other one was facing away from the pick-up, looking out on the prairie. Like he was waiting for something else.'

'For what?' Johnny said.

'Wait and I'll tell you,' Luke said. 'The white guy offers you a piece of paper with a lot of writing on it. He offers you a kettle. He offers you a gun. It's like he has all this stuff on the seat and he keeps showing it to you. A pair of jeans, a TV set, a cell phone. And every time he picks up something new I'm shouting, don't take it, don't get in the truck, let him drive away.'

'I'd take the cell phone and the jeans,' Dean said.

'I'd take the gun,' Johnny said. 'I'd blow the asshole's brains out and then I'd get everything.'

'Don't take the gun!' Luke shouted suddenly.

From out front they heard Jubal's voice. 'Hey! Cool it back there.'

'Whatever you do, don't take the gun,' Luke said, lowering his voice. He was out in a sweat, and shivering, like he had a fever. Johnny looked at Dean. Dean looked at Johnny. 'It's okay, bud,' Johnny said to Luke. 'I ain't going to take the gun.'

'The other one of you,' Luke said, 'is still over on the roadside, waiting. And now there's someone coming. It's a rider on a horse. An old warrior, painted up and wearing a war bonnet and everything. But I can see right through him, like he's made of air. He's a ghost. And he stops his horse and looks down at you and for a long time he doesn't say anything. He doesn't offer you anything because he ain't got nothing to offer. And then he speaks.'

'What does he say?' Dean asked, after Luke hadn't spoken for a few seconds.

'He says a time is coming. All the ghosts are coming back. The buffalo are coming back. The deer and all the other animals are coming back.'

· 'Oh man,' Johnny said. 'Is that it? Is that your prophecy? We had this a thousand times before.'

But Luke Stands Alone didn't seem to hear him. The sweat poured off him, and he just kept on talking, as if he were the old ghost warrior himself. 'The uranium is going back into the earth,' he said. 'The garbage is all going back to where it was made. The cars are going, and the missiles and the pollution. People don't know how to live in harmony with the earth. The wasichus never knew how, and most Indians have forgotten or been killed for trying to remember. But a time is coming. Don't get in the car with that old man. Don't take any of his gifts. Just wait. Don't forget who you are.'

Luke stopped, and for a minute nobody said anything. And then Luke wiped his face and said, 'And he rode off across the prairie. And I looked and the road wasn't there any more. The pick-up was gone, and so was one of you guys, but the other one was still standing, staring out at nothing.'

'Goddamn ghosts,' Johnny said.

Luke put his head down on the table. It didn't take much to get him drunk, but he looked more exhausted than drunk, as if the vision had taken all his energy out of him. In a minute he was asleep.

Johnny looked at Dean. Dean shrugged. 'Well, just because he stopped drinking don't mean we got to,' Johnny said, and he called on Jubal.

Jubal brought them more drink. He jerked a thumb at Luke. 'He can't sleep in here.'

'Looks like he's doing it fine,' Johnny said.

Jubal said, 'I'm saying he can't sleep in here. You can take him out back and he can sleep it off in one of the cars in the yard. Five dollars for the privilege. For that he even gets a blanket.'

'We'll be going soon,' Dean said. 'Just leave him be, won't you? We're your best customers.'

'We're your only customers,' Johnny said, 'and we ain't going yet.'

'He can't sleep in here,' Jubal said. 'Either you take him out to the yard, or you put him on the street, but he can't stay there.'

'It's going to be a cold night,' Dean said. 'He might freeze. He might not wake up again.'

'That's why he gets a blanket,' Jubal said.

'Leave him till we've finished these beers,' Dean said. 'Then we'll move him.'

Jubal retreated, muttering.

Johnny said, 'I'm drunk. Maybe we'll all sleep in one of Jubal's old wrecks.'

Dean said. 'Give me your key, man. I'll drive. We'll buy some more beers to take with us and we'll get Luke in the car and we'll drive a little ways and then we'll pull over. We'll have another drink and then if I can't get you to my place we'll all sleep in the car. That way we'll keep warm. There's snow coming, Johnny. We ain't leaving Luke alone, here or anywhere.'

'I didn't say we would,' Johnny said.

'We'll have sweeter dreams in your car than in Jubal's yard. Indian dreams.'

Johnny put a hand on Luke's back. 'Do you think he's dreaming about us now?'

Dean laughed. 'Yeah, I think maybe he is. I think he's looking out for us, so we got to look out for him.'

They finished up, and then they hauled Luke through the front room of the bar and out to the street, which wasn't much of a street, just the road with the bar alongside it and a sign that said MAIN STREET. Jubal looked like he'd never seen such a thing in his life, Indians leaving the Buffalo Saloon in a state of semi-sobriety, but he didn't try to persuade them to stay. Maybe he was as tired of it all as they were. Maybe he knew there'd be another party along soon enough.

They slung Luke in the back of Johnny's car and Johnny gave Dean the key and went back in for a six-pack.

Luke didn't stir.

Dean stood in the road, feeling the chill air, watching the snow-lined hills fading into the dusk. Far, far off he thought he saw the lights of an approaching car. Then he didn't, and there was nothing but darkness gathering around him.

The door of the Buffalo Saloon slammed, and Johnny staggered over.

'Hey, Dean,' Johnny said. 'You all right, man?'

'I'm good. You all right?'

'I got some more cans. We're going to be fine. Hey, Dean, what do you see out there? You see something?'

Dean watched a few moments longer. The sky was clouding up. There were some stars, but they weren't going to last.

'I don't know,' he said. 'Maybe I do. What do you see?'

Johnny stood beside him, the brown bag with the cans in it under one arm. He put his other hand on Dean's shoulder, to steady himself, and they peered into the night together for a long time, not saying anything, while, on the back seat of the car, Luke lay sleeping like a child.

# LOS SAN PATRICIOS

*by* RODDY DOYLE

THE WRITER HAD a new book out and he was touring America, a city a day, a reading a night. He'd fly to a different city and hear the same questions – 'Do you use a laptop?', 'What other Irish writers do you like?', 'Why do you think the Irish punch above their weight, literature-wise?' But then there was a new question that quickly became one of the same questions: 'Have you heard about the San Patricios?'

He had, in fact, heard about the San Patricios. The Chieftains and Ry Cooder had a new record, called *San Patricio*. There'd been an article in the *Irish Times* about it and he'd read the first paragraph. The San Patricios were a group of Irishmen who'd changed sides during the Mexican-American War of 1846 and '47. That was as much as he knew. But it was enough, he thought, to let him answer, 'Yes'. One delighted man stood up and said, 'Can you believe those guys?' A woman in a different city spoke about the Irishmen who'd decided to fight with 'their Mexican brethren'. Had the writer, she asked, ever considered writing about those men?

✕

–Fuck sake, man.

Rex had no idea where he was. He wasn't even sure he'd woken up. It was hot, and he was outside. But they'd been inside, under a ceiling, when his eyes had started closing. He wasn't sure but. Nothing was clear or coming back to him.

–Clueless?

He put his hand over his eyes, to block the sun. Clueless – real name Trevor – was lying beside him, just starting to move. He was covered in red dust – everything was red. The ground shook. The noise was unbelievable, some kind of explosion.

–Clueless?

–Wha'sup?

–Where are we?

–Haven't a fuckin' clue, man.

Clueless sat up and looked around him. New dust blew into their faces.

–We're hallucinatin', said Rex.

–That's it, said Clueless.

Several men ran past. Their boots threw more dust and grit back at them. The men were carrying rifles.

–They're all dressed the same, like. Look.

–Cunts.

One of the men fell like he'd just been thumped. He hit the ground as they heard the gunshot and saw the quick spurt of blood slap the earth.

–Did you see that?

–Yeah.

–We're havin' the same hallucination.

–Brilliant.

–That stuff is ace, man.

Rex remembered now. He'd been smoking the stuff, Smoke XXXX, with Clueless and Clueless's brother, in their bedroom. The brother, Eliot, had got the Smoke – 'Warning: Not For Human Consumption' – in the local head shop, three days before the law had shut it down.

–Where's Eliot?

–Over there, said Clueless. –Look it.

Eliot was lying dead a few yards away. His body was partly hidden behind a red boulder. They couldn't see his head but the Converses were definitely his.

–Fuckin' amazin', said Rex.

–How come he's not seein' the same things as us? said Clueless.

–He smoked the four Xs too.

–Yeah, said Rex. –But he didn't drink any of the hand-gel. He spat it out the window. 'Member?

–That's righ', said Clueless.

A bullet nipped his ear and whacked a stone just in front of them.

–Fuck!

Rex was laughing.

–Brilliant, he said. –Well worth the money.

–Fuck off, said Clueless. –It's fuckin' sore. Blood, look! It's pourin' out o' me!

–Coolio.

The ground shook again. The explosion roared and shook their clothes like heavy hands going all over them.

A man in a uniform ran past. He stopped and turned – he had one of those mad black moustaches – and shouted at them. Then he ran off again.

–What fuckin' language was tha'?

–Paki or somethin'.

–We must be in Iraq.

–Yeah, said Clueless. –Come here but. Hallucinations aren't supposed to be sore, are they? My ear's fuckin' killin' me.

–Mine's grand, said Rex.

He checked his ear.

–Yeah, no blood.

He shouted after the running man.

–Here! Bud!

But he'd gone.

–Dopey cunt.

Another man came running at them. He was carrying a pile of rifles, trying to hold them all in his arms. He fell – he dived – right beside the lads.

–Sound men, he said in a bogger accent. –You've arrived.

–S'pose, said Rex.

–You're Dublin boyos.

–That's righ'.

–Well, you're great men and welcome, said the bogger.

He handed them a rifle each.

–There now.

–Coolio, said Rex.

–Where are we, bud? said Clueless.

–Where are you?

The bogger stared at them, until fresh dust made him shut his eyes.

–Lads, he said. –You're slap dab in the middle of the Battle of Buena Vista.

–Serious?

–Fighting for Mexico and the Catholic faith.

–Fuckin' Mexico?

–The Catholic faith? said Rex. –Mind your arse, Clueless.

–And boys, said the bogger. –You're facing the wrong way.

Rex turned and saw a line of soldiers walking towards him. The dust rose and drifted and some of the men fell, shot. But most of them kept moving, steadily getting nearer.

–I wouldn't mind wakin' up now, said Clueless.

–Yeah, said Rex. –It's borin'.

–Make sure those bayonets are fixed, boys, said the bogger. –The signal to charge will come any minute.

–I'm firing mine, said Rex.

He aimed at one of the advancing soldiers.

–Are they Americans, are they?

–Oh, they are surely, said the bogger.

Rex pulled the trigger and his shoulder fell off, the whole side of his head.

–For fuck sake!

–Yeh hit one.

–Can't hear yeh!

–Yeh hit one!

–Ace.

Rex aimed again, and pulled the trigger. But nothing happened.

–It's empty, he said. –Should there not be six bullets in it or somethin'?

–Hang on, said Clueless. –It's one o' them really old ones. You have to reload it every time yeh shoot. I seen one o' them in a film in me Da's Henry Fonda box set.

–Who's Henry Fonda?

–Jane Fonda's husband.

–Who's Jane Fonda?

–Don't know, said Clueless. –Some oul' one. You can only fire one bullet at a time.

–That's shite, that is, said Rex. –Is there not an app or somethin'? Here, pal! he shouted at the bogger. –What year is it?

–It's 1847, boys.

–It is in its hole.

But the bogger wasn't listening.

–At the ready, boys, he shouted, crouched.

They saw more men now, lining up beside them, their rifles – their bayonets – held out in front of them.

–Did you do history in school, Clueless?

–Sometimes, yeah.

–Who won the Battle of Buena whatever the fuck?

–Haven't a clue.

Rex looked at his new comrades, the line of thin, tired, ragged men.

–I don't think it was us, said Rex.

–No, Clueless agreed.

–We'll change sides if we don't wake up first, alrigh?

–Okay.

–But we'll stab a few Yanks first, alrigh'?

–Okay.

–Bit o' buzz.

–Ah yeah.

The bogger beside them lifted a rifle into the air.

–Men! he yelled. –For Mexico and Pope Pius!

–Fuck sake. And Jennifer Lopez.

–Here we go.

–*Erin go bragh!*

# OF ALL THE FACES
# IN THE WORLD,
# YOUR FACE

## *by* J A HOPKIN

S PEAK TO ME. Ok, if you can't speak, then sing, whisper, moan or sigh! I know you can do it! You have been keeping me up at night with your curses and imprecations! With your... your holy-sounding lullabies (yes, just like nuns at 5AM, bad breath and church varnish caught in their coifs). Also, I should tell you, you make some pretty fearful smells in your sleep. Your breath blows hot and cold!

Call this a conversation? Why go quiet on me now when I'm ready to talk, to open up my heart, my soul, whichever you want, the one, the other, even both? So don't go giving me those painted-out ears. (I know you can hear me.) Or that grimace you wear so well as if I'm the one responsible for everything bad that has ever happened to you.

Listen, that first day you appeared – or rather, that night – each breath of yours landed a whole sentence against my skin. And in this sentence each word was like a drop of dew you'd carried home from the city gardens. I'll admit it to you now: I was a little scared. I pretended to be asleep. I couldn't keep my eyeballs still. My shivers betrayed me. You must have noticed! And when you started your heavenly chanting, I could take it no more; the tears poured down my face, my pillows turned to puddles of longing. I turned away from you. I didn't want you to see me reflected in my misery. Why? Because you had only just arrived in my life and I didn't even know where from. (Though I am aware that everything nocturnal comes from underneath.) I did not want you to witness – so soon, too soon! – the delicious torment you were already exerting upon me.

In another pathetic attempt to convince you I was asleep, I turned to my other side (yes, an insomniac develops an endless assortment of sides). This is a manoeuvre usually full of despairing promise, to find cool, soft bones, a fresh patch of slumber. But still I could feel the features of your face branding my back. Or else an eyeball on both shoulder blades, your nose at my nape – like a dog that has the bone before the scent – while your words counted out my vertebrae like the beads of an abacus, or worse, a rosary.

I confess, I trembled. I repeat: I did not know who you were or where you had come from.

Earlier that day, another strange event had taken place. A large picture of my face had appeared on a board in the town square. At first, I did not know why, then I remembered a photographer had come round months earlier. He was working on a project about people from elsewhere living in this town. He was very friendly. He said it would be good for the people of the town to see that people from elsewhere were living happily here. I said I wasn't sure about the idea of 'people from elsewhere'. Or, indeed, about the idea of 'happily'. I asked him if the idea of 'people from elsewhere' still exists? He replied that yes, it most certainly does still exist, because if it didn't, then they wouldn't be having an exhibition in the main square about 'people from elsewhere' now, would they? Then he said he would send me the photograph for my consent.

He never did.

Some weeks later, when his visit had slipped from my memory altogether, my face appeared in the square: unsleeping, spotlit, presiding over cobbles and drunkards and bins, my features unmoved by passing trams, shouts, dropped bottles, the chimes of the nearby church.

That night, with you at my back, I could not sleep. How could I sleep with my 'people from elsewhere' face in the square? I wondered if I was a scarecrow or a scapegoat. And with you – whoever you were, and from wherever you were from – vigilant over my wide-awake body?

On the second day, you started your smells. First I think it was the local sausages, each one as thick as a wrist. Then I think a hint of a Turkish kebab. (Well, there's no accounting for taste.) I have to tell you, you were firing from both ends. I wondered if my weary body and head were conspiring to flush my already distraught senses. I thought of my face in the square, now in daylight, trying to produce a smile for the hordes who pass by the minute, scurrying toward work or food or encounters, or whatever else drives people to put one foot in front of the other and scurry.

I wondered: if I ask for my picture to be removed (well, I was sure I had not given my permission) then would you disappear too? Hours later, you produced other smells: car fumes, rain on waxy green leaves, dog shit (how did you manage these?), and something baking or frying, cutlets or fritters, so pungent I pictured the tenderised meat until it felt like my tongue was a rubbery chunk smacked flat by a hundred hammers. Is this how you pledged your affinity? By declaring all the body's functions, and as crudely as possible?

Yet you knew you had me. I was warmly encumbered by your presence. From your heavenly singing to your elemental smells, your voices and vapours filled my flat, my soul, my life, in the space of just three days, as if we had always been together and never again would part, for – didn't we agree? – if lovers don't promise each other forever they are unlikely to see beyond tomorrow.

On the third day, people began to look at me strangely in the street. My face bore a close enough resemblance to the picture in the square for them to recognise me, but they must have also noticed the differences: the sunken eyes, the dark circles, the anxious look of a man in torment. (Well, I no longer had the benefit of professional lighting.) Perhaps this is why they pointed and chuckled. Occasionally there was a shout, even a curse, but I tried to play oblivious.

I stopped going to see my picture or to investigate the crowd standing round my motionless mug. But we were united, my photograph and I: we were sleepless beneath the lids. Only, my picture did not show signs of stress. I had to carry them for the both of us. And for you, too, you who would not leave my flat. You who were taciturn for hours and then ridiculously garrulous, chanting, stamping, even growling towards the dark end of the day. I did not have enough ears to catch all your words, even with the additional (and larger) pair proffered by my picture.

Later that same day, I bought flowers, perhaps to celebrate my growing notoriety in the town, or in gratitude for your arrival (for after minutes of abuse in the square I fled back to your unquestioning love) and also, possibly, to banish your smells which were still dragging my senses through abattoirs and boudoirs and other places with French names that give off a sordid stink! So I bought tulips in pink and white. Daffodils, all soft ears and tongues! Little bouquets of purple violets wrapped in a thick green leaf. The flower-seller took my money, pointed to my face, then to the board across the square carrying my picture. Without speaking, she broke into gentle cluckings of mirth. I went as red as a busload of begonias.

When I got back to the flat, I laid these flowers on the floor all about you – a shrine to the living! To the loved! Other bunches I put in vases that I filled with my tears. Yes, tears were coming easily now, almost never stopping. My face in the square looked bold, never slept, never cried (yes, my chops took a whole town on the chin), so I had to do all the weeping, too. Though, as I have said, I could not manage any of the sleeping. One night, I even thought I should take a marker pen and draw closed lids on my portrait. Then at least one of us would get some kip.

Throughout you murmured to me, in words that one moment came like a spring breeze, scented with mown grass and bird droppings, or, the next moment, with all the melancholy of autumn rain falling in an abandoned hubcap – but still you chanted, and kept chanting, a mantra, a slogan, a military march? Once, miraculously, yes, miraculously, you produced at my feet, from nowhere, a curled and crispy brown leaf, and, on another occasion, a breath as harsh as winter, a smell of concrete and ash, a puff of icy air, and – hey presto! – a snowflake! All the time words and more words, of love and leaving, of adoration and meeting, a perpetual pledge, a long and sensual incantation that had me sniffing my own chest such was my drowsy, head-nodding delight – the *relief!* – of these words that weren't so much words as tiny portions of tenderness, and these kept on coming until I could not see for the tears pumped out by this heart and up through the lachrymatory glands.

When I came in from the street covered in petals and stems and the accumulated embarrassments of a hundred pointing fingers (for the whole town crosses the square), I looked like I'd had a tumble in the cemetery or been to a wedding and run all the way back with confetti caught on the tip of my tongue to tell you, yes, yes, you're the one! Oh, how many murmurs from the breath of love? A long and tender recital for all unmarried mortals! (For I was convinced this chanting must be of love.) How I loved you then as you sang of my loneliness, of all loneliness! For you made even the emptiness of yearning feel like a warm, communal sensation, made of holy water and buttercups. And despite your night-time eructations when, it's true, you transformed all your humours into fetid fumes, and despite the voices from the street you suddenly threw out in one language or another, or a snarling hybrid of many, plus sirens, baby screams, brutal vowels and breaking glass – how did you catch a whole city in your throat? – yes, despite this, and your acrid smells (thus matching your love with monstrosity), that night I slept facing you, and quietly, delicately, we managed the mergings of love.

On the fourth day, things took a turn for the worse. In the street, people were openly jeering at me, laughing, shouting phrases that turned my ears blue and made my loose tooth wobble, until I knew for sure that I was most definitely that person from elsewhere pictured in the square – though, bravely, my digital doppelganger didn't even flinch. Meanwhile, back in the flat, you started throwing up. But this was no ordinary puking, no, your vomit was of a celestial order, a stinking constellation, but terrestrial, too, for, either side of your holy sobbing and retching, you brought up pieces of paper, sometimes as big as a page from a prayer book, other times small, in tatters, but always covered in indecipherable scribbles, like a bastard hieroglyphic lacking the promise of revelation. Next came sweet wrappers, each one like a cellophane cat-tongue – and that might not have been an arbitrary simile, for what came after that? A feather! (By now, of course, I was alarmed by your diet. By your powers of in-digestion.) Desperately I tried to read messages from your puked-up detritus, to find some order or sequence that might explain everything – your origins, for example, or mine! – because by now the singing had stopped, the lullabies, the whispers, too. I wasn't sure where you had gone, or if you were going to come back. Though you had lifted me towards the heavens in terms of hope, you now left me with a heart as flat as a footprint. Yes, you abandoned me somewhere between my grievances and God.

One piece of paper you spat out was covered in full stops. Never before had I sensed the might of so many endings! Now the tears that filled my vases were tears of incomparable suffering. A sense of abandonment flowed through my blood and felt like a panic in reverse. The flowers were carnations. They died before they had fully flowered. Tell me, was my devotion not enough, my heart of so little capacity? Did you come as a blessing that concealed a fatal wound? Had you left, as you had arrived, in the midst of 4AM unfortunates, when I opened my eyes to a darkness that cracked like old paint, leaving me astonished that it is this life and not another that I am living, and that it is this country and not another that I am living in, and to see you there before me – yes, a visitation! – and surely not of my own making? Or maybe you had got wind – yes, that's the term! – of the word in the street, of the way people were treating me, shouting at me to go home, yes, maybe you wanted to join the herd and treat me the same way?

On the fifth day, your foul mouth found its range. I have never heard such furious curses, such mutant oaths! From what stinking orifice did you pluck your rancid tongue? There was nothing I could do to appease you, nothing to staunch the torrent of obscenities. I experienced all the pain of a loved one's scorn. Everything I said was wrong, and only angered you more. Everything you said was a condemnation or a painfully sarcastic retort. You savaged me. When once you had raised me to the stars, you now dragged me down to the sewers.

On the sixth day, the first of a new month, the landlord came round for the rent. When I opened the door of my flat, he stuck a finger under my nose, laughed, and brushed straight past me, his finger now pointing to the ceiling. And then he saw you, the condition you were in – which I had assumed to be happiness. Elation! The ecstatic negligence of love! He asked had there been some trouble? A party? A fight? Some hooligan episode? 'Everyone in town is talking about you,' he said. 'What have you done here?' Then, louder, 'What are you doing here?' And he gave that last question such emphasis that it was clear he meant, or it was clear that he wanted me to take it to mean: what are you doing in our town, in our lives, in our neck of the woods? 'Really, this is your last warning,' he said, his finger now pointing to you, my love. (Though, with equal veracity, he might just as well have said it was my first warning.)

Though you were mercifully silent, I could feel your contours cringe. He asked me, as he crouched beside you and stroked you, with a slight wince that could only hint at your frown, 'Are you a madman or a drunk?' With an angry arm, he flicked up a hundred petals that lay scattered across the floor. He asked: 'How in God's name did this happen? Is this how people behave where you come from?' He put his hand inside the hole in the wall that I had taken for your face. I waited for you to scream. But, again, only silence. I tried to tell him, no, I am not drunk, no, I am not a madman, no, people do not behave like this where I come from, though I was not clear which behaviour he was referring to, and even less clear about where I was from, though I did begin to wonder if I'd been all there in the head (if not the heart) when you and I had come together that ludicrous or benevolent night.

Standing up, the landlord laughed from his Adam's Apple to his ankles; he looked like he'd been suddenly covered in bubbles. He wears expensive sunglasses and goes boating at weekends. Last year he divided one flat into three. Only the external walls are real, the rest are partitions of plaster and wood. For months, I have been living inside one of these boxes within the original flat, like a rabbit in a segregated hutch, or a keen mind in quarantine, and then had come the sudden revelation, the blissful torment of the senses.

You.

'It looks like a boot print,' said the landlord, crouching again, and giving the hole, your face, my hope, one last stroke. 'But from the other side. And a bloody big boot at that!' He turned to me, and assumed the tone of someone addressing the village idiot. 'Why did you let them put your picture in the square?'

I told him I had never agreed to let them put my picture in the square. He said maybe they put pictures of 'people from else-where' in the square to encourage people who don't like 'people from elsewhere' to find the 'people from elsewhere' and give them a bloody good kicking. I said I didn't know anything about that, but a lot of people who are not, or who appear not to be from elsewhere, have sworn at me or looked at me in a funny way, or pointed and laughed and jeered, or shouted at me to go home.

Two hours after the landlord had carried his shaking head out of the flat (as if the ensuing dizziness was a small price to pay for shaking out all that disbelief), a decorator arrived with a pot of wet plaster. He did not point at my face and laugh. Instead, with his index fingers, he drew a rectangle around his head, and then put his smiling face in the frame. I pretended not to notice, even though I could see his chin poking out of the parameters. Then he told me that my picture was that very minute being taken down from the square. Those unblinking eyes would at last be able to sleep, to turn away from the scrutiny of the people not from elsewhere, however long or short their hair, however big or small their boots.

It took only twenty minutes for the man to cover up your face. 'A big boot!' he said, 'a big kick!' And he stood up to demonstrate what a big boot and a big kick look like. Then you were all but gone, patched up, leaving a surface as rough as a shaved scalp, you who came or who was sent to take away my longing (or to deepen it), to cause my paranoia (or to cure it), to make me feel at home (or hated). As my sleepless face was ridiculed in the square, you sang to me of love and tolerance, while blowing your breath by turns sweet and stagnant upon me. (I can forgive you your terrible wind; not one of us is perfect! Though, of course, I cannot find fault with your form: an entry and an exit, what more does anyone need?) Yes, my permanently smiling-scowling love, your sweet harsh face was banished, leaving only two faint lines where a personal prejudice (for isn't that what love is?) had made its point.

My flat is now full of dead flowers and the water in the vases has turned bad, for even tears lose their purity, and it was while sweeping up some disembodied daffodils – as if a whole season, a whole heart had died among them! – that I found a note, and before I had even read it I knew it was from you, because it was on a similar page to the ones you had puked up when you were bringing forth a city, or something else so bad that you couldn't keep it down, so I skipped nervously around the flat, first finishing the tidying for I couldn't decide whether I should read this note or not. I had such mixed feelings about these last few days. I was thinking of packing up and leaving.

Glimpsing the paper I saw legible words and that was a first, even for you – though I was convinced already of your human aspirations (or should that be divine? Yes, whose side are you on?) – even if you could no longer sing, or lick the cleft of odious curses.

Finally, when the flat was washed and scrubbed and dusted (yes, a good clean can be just as effective as buggering off) I collapsed upon the bed, a few putrescent petals pressed to my sweaty forehead, my lips close to the spot where you, my vicious-beloved, had prospered, and I ran a finger down one of your lines (how time runs circles round our vanity!), the plaster still damp on your face, and I took your note from my pocket and, with trembling hands, and a heart I had to squeeze for hope, I smoothed the paper across my palm.

'Later, you bastard,' said the note. 'We will be back.'

# ANOTHER COUNTRY

## *by* MARGO LANAGAN

'CAN YOU TAKE me to Anna's tonight?'

He stands in the kitchen doorway. His look says, *Not that I care or anything*. That terrible hair all the boys have right now, it makes them look as if they've just come in from a howling windstorm and not quite straightened themselves out yet.

'I suppose.' I'm ashamed of how small and squashed my voice is.

'Thanks, Mum-ma,' he brays, loudly and cheerfully so that I can't back down. He turns on his heel back to his room.

The artillery's very loud tonight in the east, a rolling rumble with never a break. If you didn't know what was being done, it might be a comforting kind of sound, like having your ear to the chest of a snoring dog – or even a snoring *husband*; think of that. You might mistake it for traffic, an enormous motorway full of what the boy used to call *monster-trucks* trundling back and forth, changing gears, racketing air brakes, revving their engines just for the hell of it. I wouldn't know what to do without the noise now, it's been so constant for so long. If it fell silent, I'd worry. I'd get edgy. *What are they up to?* I'd wonder. *What have they got up their sleeves for us now? Are they ramping up? Where will they start in again?*

He's *singing* in there as he digs in the mess for whatever he needs, singing along with that tinny transistor radio he uses now that the networks are down. It's awful, that underground station he listens to – the music's relentlessly offensive, and the announcers can barely string a sentence together. But the fact that it keeps playing, in this mess of a half-existent city... If I ever feel anything like hope it's because of things like that, the kids just *going on*, propelled by a core energy I can't seem to summon any more, *doing their thing.* Even *having* a thing. How do they do it? Myself, I'm reduced to sheltering and getting food and such, keeping us going just bodily; that takes enough out of me. I look at my son and want to apologise for bringing him into this life, this time and place. I don't do that, of course, I don't say, because he has no idea, really, that everyone's life wasn't always like this; he's been stepping over rubble and bloodstains and shards of glass all his life, falling asleep to gunfire and waking up to it again in the morning.

'Have you got money, Mum?'

I look him up and down. 'Is it a costume party?'

'Kinda.' He shrugs at himself and looks at me through the money-question.

'Some,' I say. 'As long as you're not shouting a big round of drinks.' That's kind of a joke; he's not drinking age yet. But then, what bar would be together enough, would care enough, to card him?

'It's just for me.' He and Anna are good like that, each paying their own way. And they're very fair-minded about the transport, too; Chas or Gracy bring Anna across just as often as I drive the boy over that bridge.

I slide out some raggy notes, pick through my coin-purse for the yellows. 'That be enough?'

'That's fine.' He always says that; I check his face to see if it really is. It is. 'Thanks, Mum-ma.' He looks at the money, not at me. That's the way we do it, now that he's a teen and cool. I love every spot of him, every ragged fingernail, every stripe of hair across his forehead.

Back to his room he goes. More burrowing, more banging. I concentrate on scouring the porridge-pan. I have to do it in this poor light now, whereas I used to wait for daylight so as to be sure to do a proper job. Oh, the things I cared about! How clothes *looked* instead of how they would wear; what people thought of me, instead of who might save my life, in a pinch; how to occupy myself some summery weekend full of garden scents, when I was free of school, or of work. What I'd do for a job now, for anything like a job! What I'd give to wave my boy off to a real school every morning, through silent sunshine!

I busy myself so as not to sit and feel frightened. With our little dark crammed-full home, I can fiddle and tidy and rearrange forever, though I can never clean it properly. Little cleanings, I can do: this pot, the useless sink and splashback, the shelf-top with the ornaments. But the dust. There is no point. The air settles and settles from the endless rumbling, and the filth with it.

'You ready?' He appears again, with his bag. A big rumble comes then, and everything shakes. The glasses ring together on their shelf, sounding alarmed.

'Let's go, then,' I say, not too briskly. I weave my way out through the clutter and snatch the keys from the drawer.

Down and down the fire-trap stairway we go and out the bottom into the car park. I un-padlock the roller door and he holds it up as I take the car out, lowers it for me to come back and lock. It's the safest part of any journey. I wish this was all in reverse order and I was bringing us home.

'Very well.' We belt ourselves in. I hardly know why, but that's what I was taught, and that's what I've taught him, so that's what we do.

It's dusk – it's always dusk. The sky is low and puffy, orange to the east where all the action is. We drive that way for a while. There are no new hazards since last time; I skirt that crater at the corner of Nancy Street with a coolness I wouldn't have believed the first time I did it. *Ohmygodohmygod*, Leanne said, peering out her window into the hole as I scraped along the wall, and then we got the giggles with relief for a good ten minutes afterwards. Leanne. Yes.

'Is it a party, then?'

'It's a *gathering*.'

'Ah,' I ladle on the false tranquillity. 'So only a *few* of you getting together and taking hard drugs.'

'Yeah. Just me and Anna and Felix and Erin. More to go around, that way.'

'I don't need to worry about you, do I.' I can spare him a glance even as I dodge the car bodies and concrete barriers and rubbish heaps. This is not even a conversation; this is ritual noise to hold back the fear.

We turn and drive down Sniper Alley, which is quite a cheerful place these days, all the little braziers, and the plastic tents shining and rippling in the drafts. Someone runs alongside us. 'Take me to the Maxiplex!' he bellows, beating the window. 'I wanna go dancing!' And he falls behind. The beauty of having a teenage boy? You're not afraid of teenage boys any more. Well, not that sort – harmless hoodies with a bit of home-distillery in them.

I go slowly along beside the canal, pretending I have to take care. Up ahead, the bridge isn't really glowing, or pulsing – that's only in my mind. It's just a grey arch in the greyness, over an S-curve of water bordered with rubbish and who knows how many rats. The S is bright with orange sky reflection. It leads your eye to the sky – *that's* pulsing, with the glow of someone's neighbourhood exploding, someone's apartment block, someone's mosque or museum, someone's day care centre or bunker or homeless camp. Smoke drifts across the orange.

My boy is humming beside me, just below the engine noise. Unless there's a big bang that scares everyone, this is as much nervousness as he ever shows; he goes still, stops joking and hums.

'Okay?' I turn onto the bridge, and his humming stops.

A man in a good black coat is walking from the other end. As I slow, he slows. 'You can see he's steeling himself,' I say.

'Doing a run-up now,' says the boy.

But the man is only striding fast, not running. His eyes are trying to fix on the Catharsis, but there's nothing to see. When he hits it we see, though. His face pales and flattens as if struck by a gust of wind or a wave of water. His hair flies up off his brow, his coat and trousers flap wildly. He keeps his eyes and mouth closed, concentrating, determined. He pushes through to our side. His self and body and clothes slip forward around him again.

'Oh, it's going to be so *uncomfortable*!' The boy pretends a little tantrum beside me, stamping his feet, pounding his knees with his fists. 'It's horrible!'

I touch his arm and slow.

'Keep going! Don't stop,' he says. 'Let's get it over with.'

'You're sure?' On the other side, the grey and yellow buildings are just as grimy as ours, the streets no clearer and in no better repair. To all appearances, it's the same place.

'She's worth it.' He's staring ahead beyond what we must pass through. 'Anna Anna Anna.'

'Hold that thought, sweet boy.'

×

Some people have to go through this every day. That man was probably one of them, the way he ignored us, his business-like approach, his quick recovery – look at him striding on past us, relieved, only a bit dewy around the eyes.

I hardly ever had cause to go through when my boy was little. Once we had to get him across to the Children's Hospital (Axel was with me then); another time a school friend who had moved there invited the boy to a birthday party and I couldn't talk him out of it.

The *Tharsis*, he used to call it. Axel corrected him, but the boy misheard again, and for a while called it *Thukkatharsis*, and he was still calling it that when Axel and I split up. Then the world took Axel away from us completely, and the word, the wrong word, was for a while one of a chain of mistakes that had caused that ultimate wrong thing, the demolishing of our little trio, which had held life steady and safe. I never minded the boy saying *Thukkatharsis*. I rather liked it; I thought it captured something of the feeling of going through the thing. But someone at the school set him right, and laughed at him. He came home and accused me of letting him embarrass himself. *I knew you would work it out some time, my darling*, I told him. He had the tiniest sulk in the world, but we both knew we had bigger fish to fry – and the schools were closed right around then, so it hardly mattered what anyone there thought of him.

And then he met Anna. At first we had networks and it was easy for them, Skyping and chatting. They were happy crossing once a week – so, once a fortnight for the escorting parents. Then everything went down, and the snail-mail just didn't cut it with the young ones. They were in deeper by then; they *needed* to see each other more often. And so we took them. And so we take them.

It hurts, of course; it hurts like being blown apart cell from cell, then reassembled very quickly, very roughly. Worse than the pain are the changes of pressure; suddenly you're afloat, completely unbalanced – where is the sky? *Is* there a sky, or a ground? And then you're being crushed from every side; you can't take a breath, and it all hurts. But worst is what happens in your head, the funnelling feeling, the rushing-through of the *stuff*, memories, dream-matter, old fears new fears and fears yet to attack, forgotten ecstasies, hoped-for wonders. All of this is brilliantly coloured, harshly detailed – but fast, too fast. And sharp edged. It's like having your brain clawed out of your skull by some creature in a desperate hurry.

Because they're young, Anna and the boy recover fast. But there's only one of me, no Axel to share the load, or to talk things through afterwards. For me the blow is a blow, every time. It's never the small price I'm paying to see my love, to touch her, to walk alongside her awhile, in whatever costume, with our other-side friends.

✕

It's best to kind of *jump* through, then to brake straight afterwards and proceed slowly off the bridge. The bridge itself is always safe and clear; no one likes to hang about near this thing.

My boy has taken it badly this time; he's come as close to crawling into my lap as he can, the gearstick poking up at his hip, one foot in its ragged sneaker jammed up on the dead CD player. He's crying, and crying out, on my thigh. I stop the car for a moment and wipe my eyes, wipe his, pat his scungy hair, rub his bony back.

'Those shoes,' I say wetly. 'They hardly *exist*! And I can smell them from here!'

'I *love* these shoes,' he says, and I know he's coming good.

I laugh at him, scratching his warm scalp. 'There's more hole than shoe, look at them!'

He hides the shoe from me, back in the footwell, and sits up, clearing away tears from his eyes as if they were just bothersome water. The look between us, the puff of air, the dropped shoulders – he thinks it's done. And perhaps it is, for him.

Anna's flat is a little farther from the bridge than ours is. There's some kind of festival on; young people fill the streets. Quite a few boys are dressed like my son, in the chopped-off black pants and jacket with the stiff white shirt-front. Where in this filthy world did they find such brilliant whites?

'What is this?' A pack of them saunters past, laughing. 'What's it to celebrate?'

'It's a band,' he says. 'It's what the band wears.'

'Oh, so these are all headed to the Stadium? No, they can't be.' I can't *remember* the last time a concert was allowed there.

'There are just gatherings everywhere, Mum. To celebrate a big gig they're playing in New York. Everyone's making their own little concert.'

We thread through several more trails and gangs of fans. 'Popular band.'

'Popular because they're the *best*.'

'Would my son follow anything less?'

I pull up in front of Anna's. Before he gets out he gives me one of his big angular one-armed hugs, kisses my cheek with his only-just-scrapy face. 'Thanks for driving me, Mum,' he says. 'You be careful, going back through that ol' Tharsis.'

'Don't you worry about me. I'm a tougher chook than I look.'

He unfolds himself from the car and goes. Anna meets him at the bottom of the stairs, hugs him, waves to me, gathers him in. When their feet step up the stairs out of view, I drive away, drive back, through the concert-goers and other hazards. At one crossroads another car comes from the other direction, and it's funny – we revert to the rules, pulling each as far left as we can, and he indicates right and waits for me, and I drive on past him, and for a moment we're back in the old world, full of the old courtesies, prosperous, easy, clean. My boy will never know that world, except for what I tell him – and why should I want him to, if he can't have it? It's much better for him to be managing in this funny feral here-and-now than to be yearning for what's gone.

I turn onto the bridge. I'm already leaking and mopping a bit, leftover tears from last time, that I held back while I had the boy with me. I pause and breathe and look through the nothing-to-see, to the ordinariness of the other side. However happy I know he is, I hate having this brute of a thing between us, this invisible violence on people who just want to get to work, or visit a friend, or walk the other side of the canal for a change. One day I'll throw a pillow and blankets in the boot, and when I've dropped him off I'll find a quiet place on this near side and sleep the night in the back seat. Plenty of people camp out in cars. No one would notice, least of all the boy.

But that's the Catharsis talking, its proximity and my fear. I lift my foot off the brake and creep forward. I'll take it slowly this time. I'll glide through and feel every burst and crush, every regret, every dazzling claw-mark on my mind. Then when I'm through, I'll get off the bridge and pull over and park. There's a whole box of tissues in the back footwell. I can cry for as long as I need to.

# PARTYTIME

## *by* ROBIN ROBERTSON

Y OU WERE QUITE the vision last night
I remember, before my vision went.

And I was left,
instead,
with this
falling corridor of edges,
the greased slipway
and its black drop: that
glint of fracture
in the faces, in the disco-ball's
pellets of light,
in the long whiskies I threw back

short and hard.
Streeling I was, and streeling I went
through some heavy gate
I came across –
and left the world on the other side, the dark
slowly calving over me
on the white slope,
on the sledge of night.

You liked my sensitive hands, you said,
but my hands are empty.
I will give you everything
but have nothing to give.

And now: now
I'll fall back
on instinct, compass,
the ghost in the sleeve,
find my way home to a place
so small I can barely stand.
The city has flooded, emptied,
flooded again.
I don't know where I am.
*Your door is near*, someone laughed,
*just around that corner.*
Pulling my jacket tight, I went on.
The frightened boy
climbed out of me and ran.

# FROM MY VOW

### *by* JEN HADFIELD

*The Mexican ex-voto and the secular-sacred in poetry*

## I. THE WITNESSED MIRACLE

*From Francisco Trujillo...*
*Candelaria Arreola...*
*Miss Josephine Rivera...*
*from the place where you find Braulio Barrientos...*
*Al Señor de los milagros...*
*To our little mother...*
*our most mysterious...*
*the holiest Virgin...* [1]

B EFORE I BEGIN to describe my research visit to Mexico, in the Año Nuevo of 2008 (an account that will reveal that I'm a terrible traveller, being neither courageous, resourceful, social nor spontaneous), I need to deliver a little spiel on Mexican devotional folk-art, in particular, the ex-voto.

This is a votive painting on a small rectangle of tin, reliably possessing a trinity of consistent elements. First, the image of the holy person, generally cushioned by a nimbus of stylised light, occupies one corner of the upper part of the ex-voto. The remaining space is shared by the retablo scene – the depiction of a calamity in which a person finds themself at the moment of the saint's miraculous intervention – and an explanatory text:

> I began to pray your novena, and I hadn't even finished when he returned...
>
> For having saved me from a Texan who tried to carry me off...
>
> I ask the Lord of the Conquest that he allow them to give me my liberty...
>
> When the bandit struck me with a dagger, I thought for sure I would lose my life...

The retablista, the artist commissioned to create an ex-voto, strives for as faithful and dramatic a depiction of the miracle as possible. He quizzes his customer for specific visual detail, but he may also take liberties with space and time, in order to best convey the vulnerability of the victim, the extremity of the crisis, the potency of the miracle.

This gives a sort of sci-fi quality to some ex-votos, as in that of M. Esther Tapia Picón (from the Sanctuary of San Juan de los

Lagos) who gives thanks to the Virgin of San Juan for saving her family from the migration authorities.

Here, the retablo scene shows the family crouching behind a flimsy shrub in an exposed, arid landscape. The perspective is dream-like, suggesting the viewer crouches with the family and experiences their predicament. In the far distance are city towers, with the quality of mirage. Between the shrub and the city lies the border. Two armed officers patrol it, assisted, despite the broad daylight, by helicopter searchlight. The helicopter is intimidating but the Virgin, in her own formidable lumina, intervenes between its apparent traction beam and the family of M. Esther Tapia Picón.

The customer dictates his text, the retablista acting as scribe, although Don Vincente Barajas, a retablista from Guanajuata, sometimes warns his customers that his spelling isn't very good.[2] There's an absence of formal Latin or liturgy, and the retablista rarely signs his work. The ex-voto becomes a direct line to El Niño de Atocha, or Nuestra Señora de Guadalupe, and this may explain the ambivalence of some priests to the tradition.

A customer might pay $10 or $20 for the commissioned ex-voto, depending on the scene's complexity. A simple depiction of a person praying will cost less than the rendition of a train wreck, a near drowning in the waters of the Rio Grande, or an illegal border crossing.

The text begins and ends with a formula of thanks to the saint for their intervention.

*Thank you, my mother!*
*Restored, I pay my debt...*

*She made me get better and sent me the cheque from my
accident...*
*Doy gracias...*
*Doy infinitas gracias...*

## II. MY BLASPHEMOUS PROJECT

Nailed to the walls and tied to the railings of a shrine, ex-votos
accumulate, a cloud of good news and crisis weathered, both personal and public; a demonstrative, familiar interchange between
the human and the divine.

In Mexico City, I visited formal collections of ex-votos in gal-
leries, in the Museum de Basilica Guadalupe, and in Frida Kahlo's
Blue House. Without the passport of faith, I shied away from
cathedrals and shrines, abashed by my whiteness, wealth, and
my blasphemous project. So I'm dependant upon Durand and
Massey's account of the grateful devout, as they queue to enter a
shrine, lingering to read each ex-voto, as they find a place to nail
or hang their own offering, agreeing how calamitous this event,
how miraculous that intervention.

The next time someone asks me who I write poetry *for*, I will
use the analogy of the Mexican ex-voto: the private conversation
with the saints, witnessed publicly by the people.

*This happened on November 20, 1943 at 7.00 in the evening...*
I think of the shrine walls, shedding and renewing their miraculous skin. There, the priests and sacristans have the conundrum
of deciding what to do when this anarchic array of miracles occupies all the available space. Ambivalent or not, the priests surely

accept that the *heart-felt need to hacer patente* (make known) *the miraculous results of a divine intervention* is irrepressible.

This is certainly the attraction of the ex-voto for me, as it also accounts for the nature of what I choose to call poetry, or the honest urge to make it: first, the compulsion to faithfully record and renew the present tense in language which is more spoken than written, while suffering the continual losses of the present tense[3], and second, a more secular, but no less miraculous, intervention.

When I'm making poetry, I'm simultaneously euphoric and winded with loss, walking fast, sitting for hours, working words until my mouth-parts work involuntarily, which makes me feel like some kind of busy beetle. My jaw aches and I digest badly. As I remember it...

I say intervention because without it, any intention on my part to write about landscape, for example, would be, and has always been, a hapless project. When I use the clumsy term secular-sacred, I'm trying to evoke the sensation of a kind of possession or animism. I'm not saying that I *am* possessed, I'm just saying it feels like it. I feel like a flute-of-me, through which is puffed teaspoonful after teaspoonful of animate air. A night-light burns in a scraped-out pumpkin.

I have come to Mexico to research the ex-voto because I eventually intend to create my own series of secular-sacred ex-votos. I hope to speak less to saints than to characters akin to Juan Soldado, or the murdered bandit, Jesus Malverde, or the gambler, Pedro Blanco. These are described as the *Victim Intercessors*, secular heroes who die to intercede on behalf of the people[4].

For my own project, The Lucy is a relation to Santa Lucia, who is often portrayed offering up her own plucked eyes in a golden dish, trailing scarlet tails of sinew. The Mater Dolorosa of Mexican Catholicism becomes my Mr Dolorosa.

I hope to turn a gallery into a shrine for ex-votos, representing the prosaic and profound hopes and fears of a fictional North Atlantic people. Breathless with gratitude, winded by wonder; language on their tongue, under the lip, like an ulcer; against the palate like a bean-shaped pearl, the finest that this rolling, tapping, tasting, arching, kneading muscle can form.

In Cuajimoloyas, the walls of the health centre advertise cholera, *consumptivo*. At worst, my Mexican project is intrinsically fake, rotten with privilege and intention.

## III. LUCK BE A LADY

My job is first to notice, and second to betray, the halo round everyday language, like the aura that adorns Our Lady of Juquila. I want to illuminate a blurt of spoken language as a peacock illuminates itself with its tail.

I commend myself to The Lucy, a Patron Saint of Nosy Neighbours, Our Lady of the Net Curtain.

I commend myself to The Lucy on the midnight airfield, striding below the turbines of this great ungulate, waving her beacons slowly over her head, as you'd repel a sabre-toothed tiger with fire.

I have good cause to commend myself to a Patron Saint of Eyesight. Last summer, I spent a lot of time considering the rear wall of my left eye. Every few weeks, specialists dilated my pupil, and through that wedged window, photographed my retina, cloudy with shedding cells, rosy with blood and light. They showed me the sweet peach of the macula and the supple trunk of the optic nerve, twisting through the peephole in the screen of my skull. They showed me the progress that their antibiotics and steroids weren't, and finally were, making on a lesion, a fuzzy weal on the retina.

My eye was a snowglobe shook up by the act of frantic looking. Over weeks, my sight cleared as the silt settled, leaving an articulated shadow, a private cartoon, that jinked and spun as I devoured shape, light, colour.

It gradually became apparent that I was going to be lucky but, gingered up on steroids, I could hardly tear myself away from my private cartoon, the antics of the animated protein: now, a dog, biting the base of its tail, now a springbok on a cave-wall, now Will o' the Wisp. My brain peers over it now. With habitude, a memento mori loses its power.

A Patron Saint of Lighthouses; that goes without saying.

I commend myself to The Lucy and her hundred spying satellites, Anik and Amos, Astrid and Cosmos, Doublestar, Echostar, Spaceway and Spot, whose plain names like the names of milk-cows are passed down through their generations.

## IV. I COMMEND MYSELF TO MR DOLOROSA

My obedient fear: of mayonnaise, markets, patrols of the polizio, polizio staring and getting their shoes shined. Fear is speaking and being spoken to. Fear in me is fast as flu. The taxi-driver says, *why do you travel alone?*

Feral cats fucking in the palazzio, hummingbirds plunging into blooms like syringes. The sun is hot and the shadow cold, and I haiver on their equator. And a red and white cat writhes in the sunny dirt as if she's lapped delicious poison.

A man and a woman hold each other below the dome of Santo Domingo; a girl jumps up onto a bench, and yells Papa! and I sit amongst ornamental agaves, and weep sheaves of private-public tears. What the Dominican Friars say – *it is not a time for visitors, thank you.*

Loneliness is the new, proud-little feather in my cap. I commend myself to Mr Dolorosa, Patron Saint of the Broken-Hearted.

I belong neither to the hostel and its blithe, lithe, bilingual Californians, nor the bird or vendor below the window, sadly calling *hecho hecho.*

I commend myself to Mr Dolorosa, our dear disreputable sir.

Mr Dolorosa his garland embracing the pilot, addict and smallness rabbit-flea.

The guide Evencio hurries ahead on the trail, calling back the bromeliads and herbs, the mountain mint, and the mountain rose.

I fail to hide my fear of falling. I will trickle down the rock like whey. I'm salt white cheese, queso blanco. *Cuidado*, says Evencio, as I grope the rock, in which a little cactus is lodged, like an anemone. *Tienes miedo?* He teaches me how to tell him I'm afraid.

Evencio, perched on the precipice, coaxes me up the rock with crumbs of language, correcting my grammar. Say *tengo miedo. Tranquillo... tranquillo. Bonita* – the receding blue ridges of the Sierra Norte.

The flat roofs are covered in pale corncobs, and a girl sits amidst them, stripping away the silk. An ox in a pasture of wagging spires of agave. Turkeys boggle. So do Evencio's colleagues when I attempt to say *he is a gentleman.*

Newness is the nimbus around everyday language. *Nopale, Corona di cristo, el chipi rojo.*

I perch on a rock behind the graveyard. The rock is littered with stripped cornhusks and the shells of extinguished veladores, the night-lights that are lit at graves and shrines. A road runs below my rock, and a man calls up *Tardes!* and so does his baritone donkey. *Tardes! Good evening!* I'm radiant with inclusion. *Don't fall!* he calls, *no caerse!*

---

A Dewar Award in 2007/8 funded my trip to Mexico and the resulting exhibition of secular-sacred ex-votos dedicated to fictional saints of the North Atlantic, which was exhibited at St. Anza in 2008. *Doy gracias.*

1. All italicised excerpts from ex-voto texts from *Miracles on the Border, Retablos of Mexican Migrants to the United States*, Jorge Durand and Douglas S. Massey, The University of Arizona Press, Tucson & London, 1995
2. From *Miracles on the Border*, ibid.
3. Sometimes the desire to make poetry dresses itself up in a kind of nostalgia, an ache for things not to change. It's no wonder, if poetry dwells on a natural landscape, that it appears to derive from an eco-poetic intention.
4. From *Miracles on the Border*, ibid 1.

# THE BIG QUESTION

## *by* GARTH NIX

A LONG TIME ago, as people measure time, but not so long that the stars have changed in the heavens or the rocks have turned to dust, a young man left his home to go hunting on the mountain that loomed above his village. He took two spears and a knife with him. One spear was short, for throwing, and that was his hunting spear. The other was long, and that was his fighting spear, should he meet any enemies, even though no one from his village had ever met or seen any enemies. The young man had never seen any strangers at all, and had heard only legends of outsiders who long ago had somehow managed to climb up to his home, a very high and secret valley, which lay nestled between three mountains.

Two of the mountains were permanently covered in snow and ice. The third mountain was smaller, and a forest grew from the valley floor almost to the icy pinnacle that stood in the shadow of its much taller companions. The forest was full of animals to hunt and be taken home to fill the pot.

As the young man – who was called Avel by his family – skinned his catch, he found himself looking out from the mountainside to the permanent carpet of clouds that shrouded the world beyond and below, and he wondered what lay beneath those clouds. Were there other animals he might hunt, and were there other people? Did they hunt deer, and eat venison, and raise corn?

That night he asked his mother, who was the wisest person he knew, what the world was like outside their valley.

'I do not know, Avel,' she replied. She thought for a while longer, then added, 'When I was a girl, there was a wise woman…or perhaps a wise man with a womanish voice… who lived in a cave near the big waterfall. My mother told me that this wise woman knew about the world beyond. I have not thought of her in years, or heard if she still lives. Perhaps if you go there you will learn the answer to your question.'

Avel nodded. The big waterfall was four days' walk away, at the foot of the valley. It was a long way to go to get the answer to an idle thought.

'It is not an important question,' he said, and hugged her.

But Avel could not forget his question. Every time he went hunting, and looked out from the upper slopes to the cloud-shrouded lands below, he wondered what was out there. Finally, he decided that he would go and talk to the wise woman who lived by the big waterfall, and ask her his question.

He left just after dawn the next day, bidding farewell to his mother, his brothers and sisters, as they prepared for the day's work: weeding in the corn field, fishing in the river and, for the next-oldest brother, taking over Avel's hunting grounds for a while.

Other villagers waved or called out to him as he strode down the terraced hill below his house. Avel was well-liked, for he was an amiable young man, and a good hunter who readily shared his kills when he had more than enough meat for his family's needs.

Avel reached the waterfall three days later, after an easy downhill journey with occasional stops to hunt or gather food. He had dined well on rabbits, berries and roots, and had even enjoyed his solitary nights, without the press of his family and all their noise around him.

The waterfall marked the boundary of Avel's world. The river spread wide as it approached the mighty cliff-face of the mountain, before plunging over it, down into the clouded lands beneath.

The cave his mother had told him about was under the cliff-face, on the very edge of the waterfall. Avel saw where it was easily enough, looking along the line of the cliff. But the path down to the cave followed a very narrow, very steep and very slippery ledge. It would be easy to fall, and if he did, there would be nothing but cloud beneath him.

Nevertheless, Avel followed the path down, careful to keep a handhold on the cliff-face at all times. He managed to get to the cave without incident, arriving just as the sun began to shine directly against the cliff.

Avel cautiously went inside the cave and leaned his two spears against the wall, as was polite. It was dry inside, and the floor was covered in rushes that were no more than a week old. Avel smelled smoke, and as he went further in, he saw a fire burning on a raised platform, with most of the smoke going up through a hole in the ceiling.

Next to the fire, lying on a bed of rabbit skins, was a very, very old woman. Her long white hair trailed down from the bed, and her gnarled, crooked hands were folded on her chest. Her eyes were shut, and Avel could not tell if she was dead or alive.

'Hello!' called Avel, but the woman did not reply. Avel took a few steps forward, very slowly. He was remembering stories of ghosts and spirits, and there was not enough sun or firelight to banish the shadows in the cave. Not all the shadows looked as if they belonged there, and they did not move as they should when the fire flickered or the sunshine paled for a moment.

One of the woman's hands suddenly moved. Avel jumped, his heart pounding. Still she did not speak, but she indicated for him to come forward. Avel obeyed, though he wanted to turn around and run.

'I knew you would come. Take my place, with my blessing.'

She raised her hand again, there was a rattle in her breath, and then her eyes dulled, and one eyelid drooped half-shut.

The wise woman of the waterfall was dead, before Avel could even ask his question.

Avel looked at the shadows. They seemed to him to be clustering closer, and he didn't know what to do. The old woman had said 'take my place', but he was not wise, he knew nothing beyond the everyday things that everyone knew. She must have thought he was someone else. The very old often saw things no one else saw.

The best thing to do would be to leave her here, he thought, and tell everyone what had happened. In time, someone wise would come to live in the cave, and Avel could ask his question then.

Avel left the cave. But he was too eager, too frightened by the shadows he felt were following at his heels, and as he stepped out on the wet ledge his sandal slipped. The hide strap around his ankle snapped. Avel spun halfway around, his fingers grasping at air instead of the cliff-face.

With a despairing cry, he fell into the waterfall.

For what felt like an interminable time but in fact could only have been a moment, he struggled to get a breath out of the all-encompassing water, and he flailed his legs and arms, hoping against hope that he might grab something to stop his fall. Through it all he felt a more intense fear than any fear he had felt before, a fear that was soon replaced, mercifully, by unconsciousness, as he failed to get his breath, and failed to grab hold of anything.

He went into that darkness knowing that it must be his death. So when he found himself waking, and his breath coming into his mouth, he was bewildered. Surely ghosts did not breathe?

When he opened his eyes, soft light fell upon his face, and he wasn't in the waterfall, or even in a river. He was wrapped in furs, and there were people nearby with their backs to him. Slowly, every muscle aching, he sat up. One of the people – a man about his own age – turned around and said something to him, but it was gibberish, the words all sounding the same.

'I am Avel,' said Avel, before he passed out again

The next time he awoke, Avel found himself on the back of a cart drawn by oxen. This was strange, for his people had neither carts nor oxen, but it was not the strangest thing. When he tried to sit up, he found heavy manacles of a reddish metal around his ankles, joined together by a chain of the same material. Later, Avel would come to learn that this metal was bronze, and that he was a slave. His rescuers had not dragged his senseless and waterlogged body from the river out of kindness, but because they thought that he might be a saleable commodity.

It was from the back of that cart that Avel had his last glimpse of the waterfall. It stretched up into the clouds, looking impossibly high. Later, when he had learned enough of the language of his captors to tell his tale, they would not believe he had fallen all the way down the waterfall. As far as they were concerned, the gods lived above the clouds. Avel was a liar and had simply fallen in the river, probably while trying to escape from one of the lowland villages where he was already a slave.

Slaving was not the primary trade of the group that had taken Avel: they dealt in many different things, travelling between the villages of the lush lowlands all the way down to the great city where the river emptied into the sea. It was in this city that they sold Avel, and he became the slave of a merchant whose name was Sernam, though of course to Avel he was always simply 'Master.'

For more than ten years Avel travelled as part of Sernam's household. They went across seas, through deserts and over mountains, travelling from city to city. Avel learned five languages, three alphabets and two systems of counting and arithmetic. He fell in love with a fellow slave, Hebela, and was heartbroken when she was sold and taken away by her new owner.

In the eleventh year of his slavery, Sernam's ship was wrecked upon an unfamiliar shore. Only Avel survived, for he was the only one who knew how to swim, and even then, it was pure luck that the wind and tide conspired together to bring him ashore.

Taken in by more hospitable people than on his first near-drowning, Avel once more became a hunter in a mountain forest, a provider of meat to a village both like and unlike the one of his birth. The people had different-coloured eyes and skin, and spoke a different language, and lived in houses made of mud bricks rather than timber, but beyond that, they were much the same. Avel fell in love again, with a woman named Kikali, and together they built a new house of bricks, and in time Kikali bore three children, who Avel named after his long-lost brothers and sisters of the village in the high valley.

The children grew, the village prospered, and all was well – until one hot summer day when a caravan slowly shambled in; the mules, as always, went straight to drink at the great stone trough where a spring splashed out cold, fresh water from under the earth. But there was no one leading the mules. The caravan master was unconscious astride one mule, and apart from him, there was only a boy, who was tied across the very last mule and was already dead.

The villagers who helped the caravan master down from the mule died soon after he did, coughing until they could cough no more. After three days, everyone in the village was dead, all save Avel. He had coughed, and sweated, and shouted against invisible enemies, but he had lived.

As was the custom in that village, though it was not his own, Avel carried the bodies to the sacred place on the mountain, and left them for the carrion-eating birds. It took a long time to finish this task, for he was weak from the sickness, and there were so many.

When he was done, he laid himself down with Kikali and his children, and tried to be completely still, so the birds would come and eat him as well. But even though he did not move a muscle, the birds kept circling above, and would not come down.

Eventually, Avel got up. The villagers had believed it was necessary for bodies to be eaten, otherwise they would become unhappy ghosts. Avel did not really believe that, but he wasn't sure, and he did not want Kikali and the children to linger as ghosts.

He said a farewell in all the languages he knew, and walked away.

A year later, he was a slave again. He had walked to the coast, and taken over an abandoned hut and a hide boat, and become a solitary fisherman, until the day he and his catch were taken by a galley with triple-tiered oars and a ram of green-shrouded bronze.

Avel rowed in the galley for four months. It was hard and thirsty work, for there was never enough fresh water for all the rowers. But it was this need to constantly replenish the ship's water that helped Avel escape, when the watering party he was with was surprised by raiders while they worked at a beachside stream.

All the galley's crew and guards were slain, and the slaves were taken to serve their new masters. But Avel spoke the language of the raiders, as he had learned it from his first love, Hebela. So he was thought to be one of their own, and was given weapons and clothing, and joined their band.

Avel did not like his time with the raiders. They roamed the coast, robbing and looting wherever they could, and they also took many slaves, selling them every full moon at a vast slave market on a beach, with the buyers' ships riding offshore, beyond the breakers.

It was a dark of the moon, a year or more later, when Avel managed to leave the band, sneaking into the night on the back of a stolen horse.

A thousand miles away, the horse was exchanged for a sack of sugar-cured fruits and working passage on a ship and, after a month at sea, Avel came to the city at the end of the river that descended from the great waterfall.

The sack of sugar-cured fruits was valuable in that city, enough for two horses, a cloak, a bronze pickaxe and some travel food. Avel rode the horses in turn, never slackening his pace, following the river back to its source.

He came to the foot of the waterfall late in summer. The river was low, mud extending for many yards from its banks to the central channel. The waterfall, too, seemed less impressive, its mists thinner, and the clouds not quite so high above. But perhaps, thought Avel, it was simply that he had seen so many other waterfalls now.

He had also seen many mountains, and climbed them, in company and alone. He had learned how to find a way among and through rocks, and how to cut hand-holds and foot-holds in ice with a bronze pick.

Even so, the way was hard. There was not one cliff to climb, as he had thought, but many, and here he learned how he had survived his fall so long ago. The waterfall did not plunge straight down from the clouds. There were many waterfalls, and many pools, coming down the mountainside in giant steps.

After days of climbing and backtracking and climbing again,

Avel came to the top of the waterfall. He pulled himself up over the last lip of stone, and looked out at the valley of his youth. It was exactly as he remembered it; it seemed nothing had changed. Only four days' walk away he would find his mother, if she still lived, and his brothers and sisters, and all the folk he had once known so well.

He was keen to go on, but the sun was setting, and the air was already cool. Avel had forgotten how cold it could be, up in the valley, and he was very tired from the climb. He looked again at the way he would go, and then turned about to walk along the edge of the waterfall.

It did not take long to find the path down to the wise woman's cave. It was wider than he remembered, and there were marks on the stone that suggested someone had worked to make the way easier.

Avel hesitated at the cave entrance. There were two spears against the wall, marking the presence of a visitor. Then he remembered leaving his own spears there, and when he looked, he saw the obsidian points, and recognised the patterns he had chipped himself. They were his spears, still in place after twenty years or more.

He took up his hunting spear but the shaft was rotten and broke in his hands. The fighting spear fared no better. Avel let the broken pieces fall, keeping only the obsidian heads.

There were no fresh rushes on the floor, and the bed of rabbit skins was long gone, and with it the body of the wise woman. But there was a load of dry firewood laid ready on the raised stone, with an obsidian flint and tinder by it, though Avel used his own bronze firewheel for a spark. Then he unrolled his cloak and lay down. For a little while he looked at the obsidian spear-points, turning them every which way against the light. Then he put them by his head, and within moments was asleep.

He awoke soon after dawn, the cave still dark. The sound of cautious, quiet footsteps had brought him from slumber. Avel had learned to sleep lightly among the raiders.

'Careful, grandmother,' whispered a voice by the cave mouth. It was a young man's voice, speaking in the tongue of Avel's people, the words sounding strange and familiar at the same time.

Avel sat up. He could see two silhouettes in the cave mouth. One young and straight; the other bent and old, leaning on the first.

'Who comes?' he asked. He was used to speaking in different ways now, and his tongue felt wrong, the shape of his mouth odd and uncomfortable. It made his voice more high-pitched than usual.

'We saw the smoke,' said the young man. 'And thought to see if a new wise woman had come to the cave at last.'

'I am not a woman,' answered Avel grumpily, his voice more his own. He stood up slowly and stretched, his muscles and joints aching from the waterfall climb. 'Where did you come from? The village is days away.'

'It was,' said the bent silhouette, her voice weak and shaky. She took a few steps forward, old eyes peering eagerly into the dark. 'We moved down in the terrible winter, when the river froze.'

Avel stopped his stretching. His heart felt like it might rise up through his chest and come out his mouth, and he could not speak. He knew that voice.

'I have a question,' continued the old, bent woman. 'Twenty-two summers ago, my son Avel came to ask the wise woman a question, and he was never seen again. What happened to him?'

Avel opened his mouth, shut it, and opened it again. He thought back across the years – of the joy and the misery, the happiness and the suffering, of Hebela, and Kikali and their children, and of all the people and places he had known.

'He found the answer to his question,' said Avel, as he walked forward, unable to even breathe, and held out his hands. The rising sun peered in just enough to light up his face, and he embraced his mother.

'And then he came home.'

The Elsewhere collection was commissioned by the Edinburgh International Book Festival, thanks to a generous grant from Creative Scotland and the Scottish Government's Edinburgh Festivals Expo Fund. In an innovative publishing and design partnership, Glasgow-based publisher Cargo and San Francisco-based publisher McSweeney's have produced the Elsewhere box set of four themed volumes.

EDINBURGH INTERNATIONAL BOOK FESTIVAL
*Commissioning editors*: Nick Barley, Sara Grady, Roland Gulliver
*Copy editors*: Jennifer Richards, Oisín Murphy-Lawless
*Thanks to*: Amanda Barry, Andrew Coulton, Elizabeth Dunlop,
Helen Moffat, Nicola Robson, Kate Seiler, Janet Smyth

*edbookfest.co.uk*

CARGO
*Publishing director*: Mark Buckland
*Managing editor*: Helen Sedgwick
*Thanks to*: Alistair Braidwood, Martin Brown, Rodge Glass,
Brian Hamill, Craig Lamont, Anneliese Mackintosh, Gill Tasker

*cargopublishing.com*

McSWEENEY'S
*Design and art direction*: Brian McMullen,
Adam Krefman, Walter Green
*Illustrations*: Jack Teagle
*Thanks to*: all at McSweeney's

*mcsweeneys.net*